RECLAIMING THE PIAZZA

Reclaiming the Piazza
Catholic Education as a Cultural Project

RONNIE CONVERY
LEONARDO FRANCHI
RAYMOND McCLUSKEY
AFTERWORD BY ROBERT A. DAVIS

GRACEWING

First published in 2014 by
Gracewing
2 Southern Avenue
Leominster
Herefordshire HR6 0QF
United Kingdom
www.gracewing.co.uk

ISBN 978 085244 844 1

Typeset by Gracewing

Cover design by Stephen McPhee of Ipg solutions Ltd, Glasgow

Contents

ACKNOWLEDGEMENTS.....ix

FOREWORD BY ARCHBISHOP PHILIP TARTAGLIA.....xi

INTRODUCTION: A CATHOLIC CULTURE.....xiii

Scope and rationale.....xiv

What do we mean by 'Catholic Culture'?.....xvii

Overview.....xxi

1 CONTEMPORARY CHALLENGES TO THE CULTURE OF THE CATHOLIC SCHOOL.....1

The 'Ecclesial Identity' of the Catholic School.....3

Defining 'Ecclesial identity'.....3

Living an 'Ecclesial Identity'.....5

'Ecclesial Identity and the 'Educational Emergency'.....8

Catholic Religious Education and Catechesis: Partnership in Communion.....12

Concluding Remarks.....19

2 EDUCATION AS CULTURAL RENEWAL.....25

Historical Antecedents.....26

Changing a Culture?.....27

Catholic Intellectual Tradition.....29

Education as Cultural Renewal.....35

Concluding Remarks.....41

3 MEDIA, EDUCATION AND CULTURE....47

Possibilities Offered by the New Media....47

The Media of Communication....49

The Media and Education....52

The Credibility of the Media as Educators....57

New Media....61

Media Responsibility....66

Concluding Remarks....68

4 THE ITALIAN CONTEXT....73

The Workings of the *Progetto Culturale*....74

Progetto Culturale: A New Way of Encounter....76

World of Communications....79

The *Progetto Culturale* and Education....79

Concluding Remarks....82

5 THE CATHOLIC SCHOOL AS A CULTURAL PROJECT....85

The *Progetto Culturale*: A Model for Catholic Education....86

Wider Church initiatives....90

Year of Faith....90

New Evangelisation....91

Courtyard of the Gentiles....91

Catholic Education as the New *Paideia*....92

Building a Catholic Culture in Schools....96

First Key: the Catholic University as Cradle and Guardian of Catholic Culture....97

Second Key: School, Curriculum and Culture....98

Third Key: Institutes of Catholic Culture as Sources of Renewal....100

Fourth key: Formation of Catholic Educators....102

Concluding Remarks....104

AFTERWORD: CATHOLICISM, CULTURE, MODERNITY: A POST-SECULAR TURN? (by Robert A. Davis)..............107

APPENDIX 1: Congregation for Catholic Education, *Educating to Intercultural Dialogue in Catholic Schools: Living in Harmony for a Civilization of Love* (2013)..................127

APPENDIX 2: Pope Francis, *Plenary Address to the Congregation for Catholic Education* (2014)............................175

CONTRIBUTORS...179

ACKNOWLEDGEMENTS

THIS BOOK WAS born on a flight to Rome in 2010 when two of the authors, Ronnie Convery and Leonardo Franchi, were travelling to the bi-annual social communications conference in the University of the Holy Cross, Rome. During the flight, they had a long conversation about the need to re-think the way in which Catholic education was conceptualised in the light of Benedict XVI's recent papal interventions on the subject. In particular, they wondered what these rich papal insights could offer contemporary Catholic educators.

Given that they were travelling to Italy, the discussion soon focussed on the Church in Italy's innovative *Progetto Culturale* (cultural project), an initiative which is not well-known beyond the borders of Italy. Was it possible, they asked, for the *Progetto* to act as a model, or prototype, for the Church's engagement with the wider world? If so, did it follow that the *Progetto* could refresh the wider Church's understanding of Catholic education? The initial answer was yes but it would be necessary to understand the *Progetto* from the inside before coming to a more informed position.

Over the next two years, Ronnie, Leonardo and Raymond McCluskey made several trips to Rome to find out more about the *Progetto*. While there is a substantial body of writing-including a fine website-on the workings of the *Progetto*, we believe that this book offers the first English-language commentary on its potential for other cultures.

The authors would also like to thank Gracewing for their willingness to publish this volume. Their patience throughout the writing process was much appreciated. A special and heartfelt thanks is offered to Anne Convery who read the final proofs and offered many suggestions for improvement.

St Andrew's Foundation for Catholic Teacher Education
University of Glasgow, September 2014

FOREWORD

The challenge of how best to transmit the life-giving message of the Gospel is one that has accompanied Christians down through the ages since Christ's command, 'Euntes Docete' (go, teach) was first heard by the Apostles.

Over the millennia, the Catholic Church has combined fidelity to the deposit of faith bequeathed by Christ, with creative and ever-new methods of proclamation, engagement and dialogue.

In our own era we have had to come to terms with a dramatic re-alignment in the relationship between Church and wider society. In a very short time the Christian message has gone from being the bedrock of our culture to becoming the most counter-cultural message of the age.

The rapid slipping of society's moral and cultural anchors from the rock of the Christian message requires of all Catholic educators and evangelisers both lucid analysis and a courageous response. That response cannot be clothed in anger or a misty-eyed nostalgia for a golden age. Rather it must be creative, respectful and convincing.

The authors of this volume have done a great service by bringing to the fore, for the first time in English, the insights and experience of the *Progetto Culturale* ('Cultural Project') of the Italian Episcopal Conference. This initiative, originally born under the encouragement of Saint John Paul II, was part of his visionary call for a 'New Evangelisation'. It was in turn developed under Pope Benedict's wise and sure guidance to tackle the so-called 'educational emergency' of Western culture and, in the creative and dynamic example and teaching of Pope Francis, it is engaged in that 'going to the peripheries'—both existential and physical—which marks the current era of the Church's engagement with wider society.

The need to re-propose the beauty of the Christian message-never to impose or superimpose it-is the core message of this text. Insofar as it situates much of its content in an educational context it will be a useful and interesting companion for teachers and catechists; its analysis of the links between communication and culture will mean it will find its place in the libraries of Catholic communications professionals and its wide-ranging, up-to-date and practical call for a new engagement between Catholics and representatives of secular culture will have a wide appeal.

In an age of 140-character tweets, smart phones and SMS messages, an age in which Christianity is regarded by some as a threat to freedom rather than its guarantor, this volume is both timely and welcome, spelling out, as it does, some new approaches and reflections on the eternal mandate to 'Go teach all nations' (Mt 28:19).

✠ Philip Tartaglia, PhB, STD
Archbishop of Glasgow and President of the Bishops' Conference of Scotland

INTRODUCTION

A CATHOLIC CULTURE

To both the insider and the outsider, it can often seem that the world of education is one in which a medley of philosophically and culturally conditioned ideas take it in turns to serve as the dominating ideology. We recall the rise of mass education in the nineteenth century, driven as it often was by the need to supply a properly trained corps of workers for the factories of the industrial revolution and to contemporary education which, *mutatis mutandis*, seeks to train pupils for a so-called knowledge economy. Woven within these utilitarian views of education, we can glimpse other and more radical voices which looked to education as the space in which the pupil/student could encounter the radical ideas which would lead to the liberation of the working classes from the grip of harsh expressions of capitalism. Catholic thinking on education has not stood on the margins of these debates but has evolved to address the changing social conditions in which Catholic schools operate.

In the light of the many-layered debates on the aims and purposes of education, both Catholic and public, there are, we suggest, two key questions underpinning the present volume: a) in what way can the Catholic school be conceptualised as a 'cultural project' and b) how can the Catholic school serve as the heart of the Church's engagement with modern society?

The central message of this volume is that Catholic education is primarily a cultural project. It is a means of communicating the Gospel message effectively with a view to enriching the cultural atmosphere of the pluralist society. To do so requires a deep and lasting commitment to dialogue with those who do not share the Christian world view.

In the introductory chapter, we explore first the scope and rationale of the present book. Following this, we explore what is understood by the term 'Catholic culture' in the context of Catholic schools and suggest that far from being simply a modifier added to other understandings of culture, it is a way of showing how the vision of the Christian Gospel is able to penetrate the life of the Catholic school. Finally, the overview of the chapters knits together the key arguments of the book.

Scope and Rationale

This book is designed to meet the needs of all with an interest in Catholic communications and education in schools. This broad group includes school managers and those members of the Church who are charged with overseeing the operation of Catholic schools. The Church's educational community is well served with a variety of writings on Catholic education's role in the mission of the Church.[1] The present volume recognises the contribution of this work to the general success of Catholic education globally.

Amongst the complex trends which scholars in various fields currently identify as defining characteristics of modern society in the West—Europe and North America, more precisely—is that of increasing secularisation.[2] This development might best be encapsulated in the argument that religion is being forced to withdraw from the public space into a private, domestic sphere. However, a counter-argument has developed in parallel with this idea: an argument which says that, in fact, religion is not disappearing from the public sphere in the West at all but, rather, is merely experiencing transition in terms of levels of attachment to institutional forms.[3] Nevertheless, subscription to either argument has profound implications for one's understanding of the relationship between Catholicism and modern culture. In an emerging society which is losing cognisance of Christian roots and, with it, a shared set of values and vocabulary when talking about the world, what exactly should the Catholic response be?

This volume argues that accepting retreat to a rump of self-referencing adherents—the creation of a Catholic 'ghetto', as it were, in the midst of society—is not an attractive option, nor is it likely to be sufficiently life-enhancing to the extent that Catholicism might be sustained as a basis for community in the future. Yet so often the perception can be that the Church's response to issues of concern to the world can seem rarefied, enshrined in worthy documents with a limited audience. The Western media, especially in the Anglophone world, is often mute on the latest papal or episcopal document unless it matches a pre-determined select list of subjects of 'general interest'. This book, therefore, asks a serious question: how might a 'Catholic vision' of society be articulated or lived out in such a way that it reaches out to society in general, addressing the 'hopes and joys' of people in speaking to their hearts and minds in the present day?[4] What we seek to do in this volume is to offer the Anglophone world some glimpses of educational thought from another and quite different socio-cultural context. We suggest that Italy's *Progetto Culturale* (henceforth *Progetto)* presents us with a major opportunity to consider how Catholic education can both meet the catechetical obligations it has to the Catholic community and the educational demands arising from the Catholic school's locus at the heart of such a wide variety of educational systems and related socio-political contexts.

The experience of one European country (Italy) which is, arguably, ahead of the field in addressing the issue outlined above needs to be examined. The *Progetto* is the brainchild of the Catholic Bishops' Conference of Italy and is intended to re-animate the Church's encounter with the culture of that country.[5] In the broadest terms, the *Progetto* emerged from the Italian Church's interesting relationship with the Italian state since the Second World War and needs to be examined through the prism of the teaching of the

Second Vatican Council. The more recent thematic origins are found in two speeches of John Paul II. In his address to the Italian Bishops in 1994, he proposed the building of a new Europe in line with the Catholic vision of the founders of the European Union whose deep faith inspired them to carry out their ambitious plan. In the same vein, John Paul expressed concern about the 'denial of Christianity' as manifested in a supposed neutrality in values arising from a post-Enlightenment model of life.[6] We argue here that John Paul's call for a *cultural, moral and religious renewal* applies not only to Italy, but to the rest of the universal Church.

In brief, the *Progetto* is a way of living Catholicism in the contemporary age. It seeks to make an impact on intellectual and popular culture through the diffusion of the Gospel using a variety of creative means. The *Progetto* recognises a substantial gap between the highly visible 'Catholic culture' of Italy—as manifested in the popularity of feast days devoted to local saints and the continuing visibility of Catholic religious symbolism in some public buildings—and a form of practical atheism in the actual reality of daily life. The *Progetto*'s logo of a 'piazza' encapsulates the key themes: the union of a church bell tower (*campanile*) and a public building (*palazzo pubblico*) is an image descended from the *agorà* of the Greeks.[7] The image of the piazza as the heart of a town emphasises the *Progetto*'s aim to place Christianity at the heart of society and allows the Christian vision of the human person to inform how people relate to each other in the shared institutions of public life. Of course, there is an assumption here of a traditional Italian-style Church-state relationship in which the footprint of the Church looms large in public debate.[8]

In terms of education, the Catholic Bishops' Conference of Italy has made education the key theme of its 'pastoral plan' for the decade 2010-2020. The rationale for this choice is set out in a lengthy document entitled *Educare alla Vita Buona Del Vangelo*.[9] A set of guidelines (*Orientamenti*) offers a substantial plan of action. In line with this long-term initiative, the most important publication produced by the *Progetto*, perhaps, is its volume dedicated to education: *La Sfida Educativa* (*The Educational Challenge*).[10] This deeply thought-provoking book reflects on a perceived 'crisis' in education which is exemplified through reference to a breakdown of 'traditional values' and a growing gulf between faith professed and faith lived. The analysis reflects the mind of Benedict XVI himself who has used the phrase 'educational emergency' to describe the educational reality in the West today.[11] The vision of education which pervades *La Sfida Educativa* includes but is not exclusive to the school: there are also chapters on family, the Christian community, work, information technology, the market, mass media, the world of entertainment, and sport. It is the wide-ranging, holistic view enshrined in *La Sfida Educativa* which prompts the critical 'rethinking' about Catholic education for an English-speaking audience which the present volume seeks to address.

What Do We Mean by 'Catholic Culture'?

The range of definitions afforded to the term 'culture' today ensures that its scope and meaning oscillate according to a broad and varied range of inter-related historical and social contexts. In this light, any considered exploration of what is inferred by the term 'Catholic culture' must draw on and illuminate appropriately the wider definitions of 'culture' available to us.

The English essayist and cultural critic of the nineteenth century, Matthew Arnold, offered a description of culture as the pursuit of perfection through engagement with the 'best which has been thought and said in the world'.[12] This widely-referenced comment is a suitable starting-point for our discussion as it locates culture at the heart of the human person's engagement with the world of ideas and their expression in the written word. Crucially, it reveals the human person as one whose search for truth and meaning lies at the heart of his or her identity. While Arnold's definition of 'culture' does not have an explicit reference to Christian thought, the stated pursuit of perfection resonates with the Gospel call to 'be perfect as your heavenly Father is perfect' although different ideals of perfection are competing here.[13] St Matthew's Gospel shows that Gospel perfection is the fruit of following the Beatitudes and changing one's heart in order to live a life animated by love. Arnold's desired cultural perfection seems to be focussed more on the life of the mind as opposed to a more integrated vision which unites heart, mind and soul.

This raises the interesting question of whether it is possible for a Christian to assent, even in broad terms, to the Arnoldian definition of cultural perfection. In one respect, we have to give a cautious 'yes' to this important question. The exploration of and rejoicing in the cultural achievements—artistic, medical and scientific—of the human race can be understood as the public affirmation of the Christian doctrine of the Incarnation. Christians are called to love the world but without become overly attached to the pursuit of material goods and what we can classify as overly materialistic conceptions of the human condition. This position avoids the latent danger in Arnold's work which emerges when the pursuit of human perfection leaves little or no room for consideration of other and deeper dimensions to human life.

To enlarge, and perhaps complicate, our discussion, we recognise that any understanding of 'culture' depends very much on context.[14] Turning to what is understood by 'Catholic culture', the Second Vatican Council stands as a worthy, indeed indispensable, reference point for our time. Etymologically and theologically, 'Catholic' connotes a universality which cannot be aligned with any restricted understanding of culture: a Catholic culture in its broadest frame of reference avoids too close an identification with other expressions of culture especially when such expressions of culture emerge from particular national contexts.[15]

Cardinal Camillo Ruini, a key figure in the *Progetto,* and a former President of the Catholic Bishops' Conference of Italy, drew on *Gaudium et spes* to define culture as follows:

The term 'culture' is understood in its widest and most 'anthropological' sense. This embraces not only the world of ideas but the daily lived experience of individuals and society, the structures which underpin it and the values which shape it.[16]

What does this mean and what are the implications for Catholic life of this definition of culture from a senior figure in the Catholic world? We suggest that this broad exploration of the meaning of 'culture' locates our debate in the link between human endeavour and the ideas—political and artistic—which, in a sense, civilise and bring some form of order to daily life. In this respect, any exploration of the relationship between Catholicism and culture cannot avoid the asking of profound questions about the precise nature of the link between the civilisation of the West and Christian thought.

Arguably, it was not until the Second Vatican Council that culture first found an identifiable domain in the Church's magisterial corpus.[17] This more explicit recognition of the link between faith and culture is, perhaps, a response to the cultural reality of the twentieth century as manifested, for example, in the end of colonialism and opening of the 'third world' to commercial and educational opportunities. The Pastoral Constitution of the Church in the Modern World (*Gaudium et spes*) advocated the wider usage of the term 'culture' as alluded to above with a focus initially on the human person's mental and physical achievements.[18] In this respect, it is not too far from the pursuit of perfection as proposed by Matthew Arnold, as we have noted above. *Gaudium et spes* goes on, however, to explore in some depth the link between faith and culture and proposed that human work is a participation in God's providential plan for the human race.[19] The understanding of 'human work' cannot be narrowed to mean only some form of paid employment but is actually a shorthand term for the sum of human achievements in all aspects of our search for meaning.[20] Arnold's definition of culture as the 'best of what has been thought and said' hence can be applied to human work and thus provides a point of contact, albeit opaque, between 'Catholic' and 'secular' understandings of culture.

The link between culture and education, while alluded to in *Gaudium et spes*, is more fully explained in the Council's Declaration on Christian Education (*Gravissimum educationis*). This important document recognises that the promotion of culture in society is the responsibility of parents and the civic authorities.[21] Interestingly, it affords Catholic schools the mission of shaping culture to the 'news of salvation' thus preparing the terrain for the emergence of a rich corpus of Church teaching on the link between education and culture.[22]

Catholic culture, so-called, is hence a way of describing the explicit and implicit effects of Catholic thinking on the organisation of society. It addresses the human person's search for meaning by offering a vision of society grounded in the mystery of the Trinity and the Incarnation. This is articulated by a positive interaction with the wider world of ideas. An authentic Catholic culture cannot lock itself behind ideological barriers, presumed or otherwise, but, in following the 'great commission', seeks to go to all nations to offer a leaven to humanity's cultural endeavours.[23] Indeed, we argue that an understanding of Catholic culture which sought to draw sharp dividing lines between the 'Church' and the 'world' would not be an authentic representation of Catholic thought.

Drawing on this vision, we suggest that a Catholic educational culture should focus on two key fields of action. First, it should seek to improve all forms of education by sharing its well-trodden tradition of educational thought with all who are concerned with good education. Catholic thinking on education, in keeping with the outward vision articulated by *Gaudium et spes*, is not designed simply as a guide for the operation of a Catholic educational system. Second, it should offer the Catholic school an opportunity to act differently from other schools and to engage fruitfully with, and 'speak truth' to, the modern state's far-reaching network of educational agencies. Given the myriad ways in which Catholicism is expressed globally, the culture of the Catholic school will reflect both the local and the international dimension and thus serve as a hub of the Church's mission wherever it is found.

Overview

In Chapter One we set out some of the principal contemporary challenges to the Catholic school. Building on Benedict XVI's claim that we are in the throes of an 'educational emergency', we first show how this diagnosis is manifested in the question of what is an appropriate 'ecclesial identity' for the Catholic school. In other words, what is the proper relationship between the Church and schools which are described as 'Catholic'? We follow this by examining closely the relationship between catechesis and religious education and show how these processes support each other as necessarily distinctive but related parts of a wider Catholic educational project.

In Chapter Two we show how dialogue is an increasingly important feature of the Catholic educational tradition. As we do not wish to live in silos, we must find creative ways to engage with the views of those who do not share our vision of life and education. This is neither the recreation of a mythical past nor the construction of a brave new vision for the future. Rather, we seek to apply the many layers of the Catholic intellectual tradition to the challenges facing Catholic education today.

In Chapter Three, we make a bold leap to claim that the partnership of new media, education and culture is a necessary blueprint for the future. Catholic education is, at its root, a means of communication: as communications media evolve, so must the Church's educational framework embrace the opportunities offered by technological advances while pointing out the challenges they pose to traditional means of interpersonal communication.

In Chapter Four, we shift the focus to the *Progetto Culturale* (Cultural Project), the Italian initiative designed to refocus the Church's commitment to influencing the culture of modern Italy. It is not our intention to undertake an evaluation of the *Progetto* but simply to suggest that it has a degree of energy and creativity around it which is both attractive and challenging. We describe the key features of the initiative and suggest that it has the potential to make a substantial impact on Catholic education in other local contexts.

In Chapter Five, we weave together the principal threads of our argument to show how the *Progetto* can act as a spur to the wider Church's educational mission. We make a bold claim for Catholic education as the new *paideia* and offer some practical ideas as the means to achieve this.

The *Afterword* sets the arguments of the volume within the context of the challenges presented to the Catholic vision of life and education by the intellectual forces clustered around modernity and the Enlightenment project. Here we glimpse the interconnectedness of these challenges which can only be addressed by a confident intellectual and pastoral vision.

There are two appendices. The first is the complete text of the Congregation for Catholic Education's document *Educating to Intercultural Dialogue in Catholic Schools: Living in Harmony for a Civilisation of Love.*[24] This document, issued in 2013, is a complete overview of the framework for Catholic education and articulates well with the present volume's call for cultural dialogue to be placed at the heart of the mission of Catholic education. The second appendix is a short speech by Pope Francis on 13 February 2014 to the Plenary Assembly of the Congregation for Catholic Education which reinforces the importance of dialogue and appropriate teacher formation in Catholic education.

Note to the text

A number of the primary Italian sources for this book have no official translation. In such cases, we have provided our own translation.

Notes

1. L. Franchi (Ed.), *An Anthology of Catholic Teaching on Education* (London: Sceptre, 2007).
2. See, for example, S. Bruce, *God is Dead: Secularization in the West* (Oxford: Blackwell, 2002); D. Martin, *On Secularization: Towards a Revised General Theory* (Aldershot: Ashgate, 2005).
3. There is an excellent summary of the various counter-arguments in U. Nowak, 'Wall of Separation? Religion's Presence in the Public Sphere of a Democratic State – Some Theoretical Reflections' in I. Borowik and M. Zawiła (Eds), *Religions and Identities in Transition* (Krakow: Nomos, 2010), pp. 119–30.
4. Vatican II, *Gaudium et spes*, 1: 'The joys and the hopes, the griefs and the anxieties of the men of this age, especially those who are poor or in any way afflicted, these are the joys and hopes, the griefs and anxieties of the followers of Christ.'
5. Website of the *Progetto Culturale*: www.progettoculturale.it.
6. Pope John Paul II, *Letter to Italian Bishops Working for Moral and Cultural Rebirth of Society* (6 January 1994).
7. In ancient Greek culture, the *agorà* was the open space in a city which served as a centre for artistic, sporting, political and cultural events.
8. A key role is given to small local initiatives in the operational side of the *Progetto*. These *centri culturali cattolici* (Catholic cultural centres) are the engines of the project and allow for a strong local dimension to apply and concretise the energy arising from the centre. Although they have a local base, the *centri culturali* are encouraged to form networks with each other and thus increase their visibility and, ultimately, their effectiveness. The TV channel TV2000 is one of the arms of the *Progetto*. It offers a varied menu of programmes all of which are informed by the *Progetto*'s unique approach to culture. The related blog *Nella Piazza* offers wide-ranging and accessible material on religious and cultural issues.
9. Translated as 'To Educate for the Good News of the Gospel.' There is no official translation available.
10. Comitato per il Progetto Culturale della Conferenza Episcopale Italiana, *La Sfida Educativa* (Rome-Bari: Editori Laterza, 2009).

11 Benedict XVI, *Address to the Participants in the Convention of the Diocese of Rome* (11 June 2007).

12 M. Arnold, *Culture and Anarchy: An Essay in Political and Social Criticism* (1869) Kindle edition.

13 Mt 5:48.

14 The many definitions of culture available to us have in common some form of collective approach to understanding how the human person engages with others to create a good society.

15 For example, the folklore of traditionally Catholic countries should not be too readily identified as expressions of a specifically Catholic culture although it is the case that many of these cultural expressions have roots in Catholic ideas.

16 C. Ruini, *Una Prima Proposta di Lavoro* (1997). The complete text (in Italian) is available at: http://www.progettoculturale.it/progetto_culturale/documentazione/00002174_Progetto_culturale_orientato_in_senso.html

17 R. J. Staudt, '"Religion and Culture" and "Faith and Renewal of Society" in Christopher Dawson and Benedict XVI' in *Logos: A Journal of Catholic Thought and Culture* 16/1 (Winter 2013) pp. 31–69.

18 *Gaudium et spes*, 53, defines culture in the general sense as referring to all those things which go to the refining and developing of all man's (sic) diverse material and physical endowments.

19 *Ibid.*, 57–60

20 'Furthermore, when man (sic) works in the field of philosophy, history, mathematics, and science and cultivates the arts, he can greatly contribute towards bringing the human race to a higher understanding of truth, goodness and beauty, to points of view having universal value' (*Ibid.*, 57).

21 Vatican II, *Gravissimum educationis*, 6.

22 *Ibid.* 8; Congregation for Catholic Education, *The Religious Dimension of Education in a Catholic School* (1988) passim; *The Catholic School on the Threshold of the Third Millennium* (1997) 14.

23 'Go therefore and make disciples of all nations, baptizing them in the name of the Father and of the Son and of the Holy Spirit, teaching them to observe all that I have commanded you; and lo, I am with you always, to the close of the age' (Mt 28:19–20).

24 The Congregation for Catholic Education is the Holy See's dicastery responsible for Catholic education worldwide.

1

CONTEMPORARY CHALLENGES TO THE CULTURE OF THE CATHOLIC SCHOOL

The diagnosis of an 'educational emergency' by Benedict XVI has brought to light the broad spectrum of contemporary philosophical and cultural challenges to both Catholic education in its many forms and to what we will describe as more 'traditional' forms of education. Benedict's thoughts accord with those of the German Jewish philosopher, Hannah Arendt, who, writing in the 1950s, had already identified a crisis in the nature of 'authority' which was manifested *inter alia* in the rejection of education (and schooling) as *loci* for the transmission of a particular cultural identity.[1] Likewise, the Catholic historian, Christopher Dawson (writing in the 1960s), had similarly identified a crisis in the concept of education as cultural transmission and suggested, controversially it seems to the modern reader, that a suitable remedy could be found in the return of the foundational study of Christian culture to the university.[2]

To be sure, the unique Christian claim that Jesus is the *Via Veritas Vita* challenges the settled will of an allegedly inclusive society which regards the possibility of ultimate truth as an illusion. In the modern secularist mindset, *truth* is what the individual feels is right in given circumstances and hence cannot be grounded in alleged moral absolutes. To claim, as Christians do, that there is such a thing as 'right' and 'wrong', with clear principles grounded in the natural law and in the insights of Revelation, is to offer an educational and cultural challenge to those who, mistakenly, see insights from religious traditions as limitations of the freedom of the individual.

This chapter presupposes that contemporary articulations of secularism, whether in the academy or in popular culture, seek to limit or remove the influence of religious belief in the public square. As Grace and O'Keefe have pointed out: 'Secularisation represents the denial of the validity of the sacred and its associated culture'.[3] In the secular mind, education and schooling are expressions of a rationalist mindset which views religiously-inspired education systems as unwelcome reminders of an unenlightened age. This challenge to the Catholic worldview and the mission of the Catholic school is made explicit when there are attempts to remove religious (or faith) schools from public provision. Implicit challenges can come from a number of diverse areas, not least the promotion of educational programmes flowing in part from a politically-expressed desire to promote an often undefined sense of community cohesion. Such curricular initiatives often seek to minimise the possibility of social and cultural fragmentation in what is called the multi-cultural society.[4] While there is much to laud in any attempt to make society more open, tolerant and free, the question of how to promote, far less achieve, this community cohesion in a multi-cultural society remains problematic: religious affiliations are visible and conceptual expressions of cultural diversity.[5]

The present chapter acknowledges that a deep-rooted secular mindset offers significant limitations to the successful operation of the Catholic school. This climate of relativism has fostered a weakening, some would claim fracturing, of Catholic school identity with the concomitant denial that there is such a thing as a Catholic philosophy of education, however difficult this 'philosophy' may be to define.[6] Within the context of these political and philosophical challenges, two selected areas offer illustrative examples of how these questions are manifested. We explore first the considerable difficulty of retaining and promoting a distinctive 'ecclesial identity' in a Catholic school in a plural society. Following this, we set out the complex relationship between catechesis and religious education in the Catholic school in order to contextualise and understand the Magisterium's developing position on this crucial dynamic since the Second Vatican Council.

The 'Ecclesial Identity' of the Catholic School in a Plural Society

Defining 'Ecclesial Identity'

It is important at the outset to offer a suitably flexible and nuanced definition of what is understood by 'ecclesial identity'.[7] Clearly, 'ecclesial identity'—when used with reference to the Catholic school—suggests an engaged and integrated atmosphere in which the traditions and beliefs of Catholicism imbue the life and work of the school. As such it is imprecise to speak of a Catholic *dimension* to the Catholic school as if there were other, perhaps competing and equally valid, 'dimensions' to the life of the Catholic school. The Catholic school is a civic institution which, rightly, should be concerned with wider educational provision and operate in accordance with the proper jurisdictions of the state. Where the challenge lies is in marrying this unavoidable public role with the obligation to provide an experience to its students which is consonant with the demands of a Catholic philosophy of education.

Of course, any exploration of 'ecclesial identity' and its implications for pastoral practices must be rooted in an understanding of developments in ecclesiology. Contemporary Catholic ecclesiology has encouraged a noticeable shift away from highly stratified 'models' of Church towards a recovery of the ancient notion of the Church as *communio*.[8] The rediscovery of *communion* has the potential to bring together the Second Vatican Council's commitment to the notion of the Church as the 'people of God' with more sacramental models such as the Church understood as the 'mystical body of Christ'.

As the Catholic school is part of this *communio,* its 'ecclesial identity' ought to reflect the theological and pastoral richness which are intrinsic to *communio.* A key element here is an openness to dialogue which, it has to be stated, is not in any sense a weakening of Catholic identity but a comprehensive and confident manifestation of the Church's desire to allow all people the opportunity to encounter Christ. In this light, the Magisterium's claim that the Catholic school has a distinctive 'ecclesial identity' opens a wide conceptual field within which many competing ideologies and policies seek to influence its life and mode of operation. At the heart of this is the crucial question of how the Catholic school can adhere to its foundational Catholic values, serve the spiritual and pastoral needs of the Catholic community and offer a rich and meaningful education to all, including those of different religious and philosophical positions who wish to attend the Catholic school. How can this be done—and what are the key challenges?

First, the provision of Catholic schooling is part of the contemporary educational landscape. It assumes many different shapes and forms across a range of cultures. Whatever the particular national and political context, Church teaching on the relationship between the Church and the Catholic school claims that the Catholic school is integral to the teaching mission of the Church.[9] The term 'ecclesial identity' in the context of the Catholic school is hence shorthand for a broad and historically-conditioned understanding of Catholic education. Its key features include (in no particular order of importance) the following: a close alignment between the hierarchy and the operation of the school; regular opportunities for religious worship; high visibility of religious symbolism in the fabric of the school; corporate satisfaction in a *distinctive* vision of Catholic education and a constant engagement with the unique philosophical and theological basis of Catholic education. In this grand vision of education, the Catholic school is a community of faith where all (staff and pupils) are encouraged, and indeed expected, to live according to the tenets of the Gospel and in fidelity to the Magisterium.[10] To move towards this goal, it is necessary to have a corps of committed and well-formed teachers who will be instrumental in shaping the Catholic identity of the school.[11] The array of faith, traditions and values which have emerged from the Catholic Christian tradition in education allows Catholic educators to serve as both good professionals and authentic Christian witnesses in the school.[12] Crucially, it ensures that the Catholic school is underpinned by a distinctive 'faith-based' vision of education which seeks inspiration from a wide range of philosophical and theological sources.[13]

Second, it is necessary to reflect further on the social and cultural implications arising from the 'ecclesial identity' of the Catholic school. Given the multiple contexts in which Catholic schools operate, and placing these within the underpinning theological principle of *communio*, expressions of 'ecclesial identity' will vary, rightly, according to the needs of the local Catholic community. This 'unity-in-diversity' hence encourages a range of models of Catholic schooling which are united by the common bond of the Church's doctrinal and educational heritage. Within this mosaic of provision, the different levels of accommodation with other providers of education present opportunities for dialogue on a number of levels. Of course, difficulties arise when Catholic schools are so enmeshed within the state system that it becomes hard to ascertain their distinctiveness both in curricular provision and in the general life of the school. It is at this point the challenge of 'living an ecclesial identity' arises.

Living an 'Ecclesial Identity'

There are many who would state that Catholic schools which are true to their mission may find themselves at variance with the state and its educational agencies. While Catholics should not shy away from robust debate in cultural, religious, economic and ethical matters, neither should they actively seek confrontation with other educational providers for its own sake. The Catholic school's confidence in its own identity can be manifested concretely in a continual effort to propose—without imposing—the Catholic vision of the human person to all of its partners in dialogue. Given the recent moves in the Church to focus urgently on the 'New Evangelisation' of traditionally Christian countries, it is important to pause and reflect on how the Church can engage in a fruitful dialogue which is both respectful of the 'other' yet retains full confidence in the distinctive Catholic vision of education.[14]

The 'New Evangelisation' presents some interesting challenges to the Church in general and to the Catholic school in particular.[15] Its key themes and foundational principles cut across, it may appear, the climate of tolerance and inclusion which are regarded as key values of the modern state.[16] The 'New Evangelisation', by way of contrast, is grounded in the notion that the religious and cultural fabric of the traditionally Christian societies of the West has been seriously wounded by the twin forces of secularisation and moral relativism. (The New Evangelisation is not primarily concerned with the traditional 'missionary' countries.) The 'New Evangelisation' will seek ways to promote a wide range of corporate activities designed to rekindle a Christian spirit, or culture, in society. The initiative is designed to allow the 'nominal Catholic' to re-engage in some way with the Gospel, leading to an encounter with Jesus Christ in his or her daily life and, crucially, in the sacramental life of the Church. The methods employed in this evangelising enterprise will, of course, vary from one country to the next depending, as always, on local circumstances and resources. It will be interesting to see how the Catholic school is integrated into this mission in the light of Benedict's statement that 'schools remain an essential resource for the new evangelisation'.[17] This important observation locates the Catholic school at the heart of the 'New Evangelisation' project and reinforces the school's 'ecclesial identity'. Furthermore, the clear integration of the Catholic school within the 'New Evangelisation' enterprise calls into serious question the school's place in a plural education system. How can a school which claims to be open to all and to respect freedom of religion and worship countenance such a close association with an enterprise with such clear evangelical aims?

These are valid arguments and merit a serious and well-considered response. A counter-argument would offer a more nuanced assessment of the link between the Catholic school and the Church's mission to evangelise. This would be focussed on how the Catholic school tailors its educational distinctiveness to meet the needs of those who are open to wider questions about God and human existence yet are not ready to respond to the call of faith.[18] Parents who choose to send their children to a Catholic school should be aware that there is a distinctive anthropology underpinning its curriculum and pedagogy. All pupils are invited to engage in a suitable manner with the Catholic message but this does not mean that any form of faith-commitment and sacramental practice will be stated as explicit 'outcomes' of Catholic schooling. This understanding of the Catholic school as a place of 'pre-evangelisation' seems to challenge less sophisticated understandings of Catholic schools as places designed primarily to meet the needs of the Catholic community. Certainly there remains some work to be done in finding a model of Catholic schooling which satisfies the many demands arising from the Church and the state. Such endeavours do not necessarily lead to a weakening of Catholic identity as such but should be seen as sincere attempts to re-shape established patterns of schooling in order to broaden the appeal of the Catholic school.

'Ecclesial Identity' and the 'Educational Emergency'

At this point we will explore how the 'ecclesial identity' of the Catholic school is challenged by the 'educational emergency'. First, we need to ask what is understood by this term? In brief, and as noted by Benedict XVI, the gradual re-imagining of the 'traditional' notion of education as a discovery of wisdom and right living in favour of an education understood principally as a preparation for work and the development of 'key' skills and aptitudes, has effected a revolution in the way schools (and Higher Education institutions) operate.[19] Again it is necessary to act with caution here as debates on standards in education are often fraught with the danger of over-simplification and the translation of personal memories into hard evidence. For example, what do we mean by a 'traditional' education? Careful study of the history of education offers a varied picture of provision: simply to place a barrier at any point in history as the dividing-line between so-called contemporary and traditional education would be an unwise and injudicious act. Furthermore, it is hard to see what is wrong with an education preparing young people for the world of work given that, in the Catholic mind, human work is a participation in the work of God and should be done as well as possible.[20]

Nonetheless, it has to be asked which cultural forces have coalesced to present what Benedict XVI has identified as the current 'educational emergency'. This wide-ranging and, indeed, highly-charged statement, merits deeper consideration by all with an interest in education. Benedict's diagnosis does not get caught up in the rhetoric of those who bemoan the passing of what they hold dear and criticise, as a matter of course, the educational and cultural levels of the younger generations. History provides plentiful examples of older generations bemoaning the behaviour, attitudes and lack of learning of the younger generations.[21] For Benedict, the current 'educational emergency' is the doleful consequence of a deep-rooted anthropology of individualism which eschews the insights of Tradition and Revelation and replaces them with a narrow moral relativism. What makes the present situation different to politically-inspired criticisms of educational 'standards' is that Benedict is actually defending the rights of the young to receive a full and mature human and religious formation: the so-called 'generation gap', he believes, is the effect and not the cause of the 'educational emergency'.[22] This seems to turn on its head the very idea that it is the 'generation gap' itself which drives the change in education towards an outcome regarded as more relevant to the needs of a younger generation eager to leave to one side the cultural and moral restrictions of an earlier age.

For Benedict, the younger generations—although a group which does not admit easy definition in terms of age—are the unintended victims of a wider crisis which has emerged from an incomplete understanding of the human condition. What is significant about Benedict's intervention in the field of education is his concern for the wider processes and conceptual foundations of education. He is not referring specifically to issues arising in Catholic schools but has widened his scope to refer to the effects of relativism on the role of the school in the preservation and transmission of a culture of truth and authentic humanism. The challenge for Catholic educators hence is to search for opportunities to engage in dialogue with those who are uneasy with or even reject the notion of an ultimate 'authority' which lies beyond the language of choice and personalisation. In this light, we need to consider what the Catholic intellectual tradition can bring to contemporary educational debates.

Catholic educational philosophy recognises the unity of all knowledge as part of the revelation of God to His people. It proposes education as the vehicle for the transmission of a particular worldview and associated culture. In this vision, human flourishing is wholly consonant with this active engagement with the bodies of knowledge which have come from the great minds of the past.[23] In contrast, other educational philosophies which favour an active 'construction' of meaning arising from reflection on experiences seem to place less importance on these insights from the past. This can often lead to a constant search for novelty, innovation and new experiences. When this hermeneutic is applied to the education of young children, it fosters a so-called child-centredness which, in its extreme form, results in a 'content-lite' education designed to minimise the role of the teacher as 'instructor'.[24] While this is a highly granular and culturally conditioned debate, and one which cannot be explored adequately within the limits of one chapter of a book, its key lines of thought have not left unaffected the operation of the Catholic school.

Within this broader cultural context, the 'educational emergency', rooted as it is in a marriage of cultural relativism and hostility to a so-called pedagogy of transmission, provides a forum in which the provision of specifically Religious Education and catechesis can be evaluated.[25] As there has been a 'crisis' in the nature of cultural transmission, so too has there been a concomitant crisis in catechesis which has been recognized by the Magisterium. The *General Directory of Catechesis* for example, constantly reminds the whole Church of the importance of the *transmission* of the Gospel message, perhaps as a recognition that catechesis had been overly influenced by educational and cultural philosophies which have challenged the value of a pedagogy of transmission.[26] It is hard to deny, however, that many baptised Catholics, including Catholic teachers, demonstrate no more than a basic awareness of the key doctrines of Christianity. This cultural reality challenges the 'ecclesial identity' of the Catholic school as pupil and staff attachment to the philosophical, theological and educational insights emergent from the Catholic faith tradition, including regular sacramental practice, is oft-times lacking.

Alongside the phenomenon of what we will describe, albeit unsatisfactorily, as the 'poorly-formed Catholic', a second reality—that of cultural pluralism in the West—has radically altered the composition of the Catholic school population. It could be argued that the Catholic faith tradition is itself pluralistic owing to its roots in the monotheism of Judaism and the rationality of the Greeks. Furthermore, the multiplicity of liturgical rites and traditions of popular piety illustrate the capacity of Catholicism to absorb and integrate other cultural traditions. In this light, the Catholic community, as a plural religious community in a plural society, is called not just to observe and comment on cultural developments but is required to participate actively in the social, political and cultural life of society.[27] While the inclusion of pupils of other religious and philosophical traditions in the Catholic school is a cause for satisfaction, the Catholic school has to find a way in which its requirement to be a community of faith—and hence called to contribute to evangelization—can be aligned satisfactorily with its role as a public institution.

To explore this further, Catholic educators would do well to think deeply about the implications of the 'ecclesial identity' of the school. There is a pressing need to refocus on the foundations of Catholic education as an enterprise inspired principally by Catholic Christian anthropology.[28] For example, when we hear of Catholic schools winning prizes and awards from state agencies it is good to welcome the effective 'PR' this affords the Church. On the other hand, to what extent do such awards sit within the mission of the Catholic school as a place to encounter Jesus Christ?

To conclude this section, Catholic schools are often lauded as examples of both a) good practice in education and b) how to raise attainment and promote a positive self-image. It remains a moot point, however, whether this public recognition has been achieved at the expense of an education rooted in the search for wisdom and the encounter with God in Jesus Christ. In other words, how deep-rooted is the 'ecclesial identity' of the Catholic school beyond the more obvious signs of religious affiliation? One way of so doing is to re-evaluate the conceptual understanding of Religious Education in the curriculum of the Catholic school.

Catholic Religious Education and Catechesis: Partnership in Communion

In the Catholic school, all curricular subjects should draw inspiration from Christian anthropology and its related educational philosophy.[29] It is, however, the specific subject of 'Catholic Religious Education' that provides the intellectual resources necessary to underpin both the Catholic school's encounter with culture and society and its key role in the wider evangelising and catechetical mission of the school. As highlighted above, the wider educational crisis has not left Catholic Religious Education unaffected.

The tension between education understood as the *transmission of a particular worldview (and associated culture)* and education understood as a personal *construction* of meaning, despite the inherent limitation of such binary language, can easily lead to Catholic Religious Education being pigeonholed as an anachronistically taught subject. By this we mean that Catholic Religious Education, as seen by outsiders, is more concerned with the passing on of an assumed uncritical attachment to a body of knowledge than to the fostering of critical thinking and the recognition of the life-experience of the student. Hence Catholic Religious Education seems to lie outside the standard curricular provision and becomes a supplement to a curriculum which is primarily driven by the exigencies of the state. The challenge for contemporary educators is to offer a Catholic Religious Education syllabus as part of a wider Catholic school curriculum grounded firmly in the Catholic philosophy of education.

The robust debate on the nature and purpose of Catholic Religious Education has definitive and well-established roots from both inside and outside the Catholic tradition. Indeed this debate is reflected in nomenclature as it could be argued that the subject titles 'Catholic Religious Education' and

'Religious Education' are only remotely related to each other. This conceptual gap is a contemporary expression of significant philosophical challenges from outwith the Catholic tradition which, starting in the early years of the twentieth century (in America) and made more explicit in the 1960s (in the UK), sought a more 'liberal' approach to Religious Education. The original vision of 'liberal Religious Education' was grounded in a commitment to the open pursuit of truth in a plural context.[30] In this new configuration of Religious Education, knowledge of religion, religions and religious ways of thinking was deemed the most democratic and educationally valid way of teaching about religion in the increasingly diverse societies of the Anglophone west. A key figure in this debate was Professor Ninian Smart whose work on new frameworks for Religious Education continues to attract comment in contemporary academic journals.[31] Smart was not a Catholic but his work did influence Catholic thinkers like Gabriel Moran and, to a lesser extent, Gerard Rummery.[32] Drawing on Smart's ideas, Rummery's seminal book, *Catechesis and Religious Education in a Pluralist Society,* laid out the reasons why catechesis and school-based Religious Education (in Catholic schools) should move in separate but connected universes. Rummery's book initiated a series of robust debates and derivative articles in Catholic academic circles in the 1980s over the scope and purpose of Catholic Religious Education particularly on whether it should be *explicitly* concerned with the faith formation of young Catholics.[33]

The relationship between catechesis and Catholic Religious Education is best framed within the following broad-based conceptual frameworks: a) Catholic Religious Education understood as a critical exploration of religions and religious ways of thinking and b) Catholic Religious Education understood as formation in the Catholic faith and hence very close to / synonymous with catechesis.[34] In analysing the key movements in this fertile debate, the following questions emerge: what is the relationship between 'Religious Education' as a specific school subject and the place of catechesis in the Church and school? Which has precedence, catechesis or Religious Education? In what way do they differ in subject-matter and pedagogy—and does any of this matter?

This debate is spread over a wide canvas. It is necessary, however, to set it in the context of the post-Vatican II Magisterial documents on both education and catechesis along with the considerable body of associated secondary literature. The weight of the documentary evidence clearly shows that far more intellectual and pastoral energy has been expended on thinking through the aims, purposes and sites of catechesis. Catholic Religious Education, by contrast, had been treated mainly in the context of broader documents on education and it was not until 2009 that the Magisterium issued a short document dedicated exclusively to Religious Education in schools.[35] The *Circular Letter to the Presidents of Bishops' Conferences on Religious Education in Schools* brought together into one short document the insights on the nature of Religious Education which had been gradually and systematically developed in the preceding thirty years. It retained the working complementarity of catechesis and Religious Education which had been a key theme of the Magisterial documents of that time:

> Catechesis aims at fostering personal adherence to Christ and the development of Christian life in its different aspects whereas religious education in schools gives the pupils knowledge about Christianity's identity and Christian life.[36]

In contrast to the reforming energy which had been woven through the wider Conciliar corpus, Vatican II's education declaration *Gravissimum educationis* was, on the whole, a modest document.[37] It had been heavily inspired by Pius XI's Encyclical *Divini illius magistri* which remains to this day (2014) the only Papal Encyclical on education.[38] Pius XI's document reflected the concerns of the inter-war years and his comments and observations, while somewhat antiquated in aspects of language and style (which is to be expected), retain value as a comprehensive map of the field of Catholic education. It seemed that *Gravissimum educationis* was more concerned with maintaining the *status quo* in education and so preparing the ground for a more forensic exploration of the Catholic tradition on education in due course. With the benefit of hindsight, we can now see that three key documents from the Congregation for Catholic Education formed a post-conciliar trilogy outlining the foundational principles of Catholic education: *The Catholic School; Lay Catholics in Schools; The Religious Dimension of Education in a Catholic School.*[39] Within the many and varied issues explored in these Magisterial documents, there emerged an interesting perspective on the relationship between Religious Education and catechesis which recognised their thematic and conceptual complementarity as well as their shared doctrinal territory. The following citation summarizes the 'state of play' in 1988:

> There is a close connection, and at the same time a clear distinction, between religious instruction and catechesis, or the handing on of the Gospel message. The close connection makes it possible for a school to remain a school and still integrate culture with the message of Christianity. The distinction comes from the fact that, unlike religious instruction, catechesis presupposes that the hearer is receiving the Christian message as a salvific reality.[40]

This is a significant paragraph in the development of post-Conciliar teaching on Catholic Religious Education.[41] It proposed *Religious Instruction* in schools to sit alongside broader catechetical initiatives, wherever they existed. The term *instruction* merits some comment as it connotes a more deductive approach to education at a time when the wider educational climate was increasingly sceptical of the value of so-called didacticism in education and schooling. In addition, the Smartian influence has ensured that the more commonly-used subject title of *Religious Education* was no longer automatically assumed to be concerned wholly or at all with any form of faith formation. The Magisterial approval of a 'split' between catechesis and Catholic Religious Education hence encouraged those within the Catholic tradition who sought to minimise the faith-development aspect of Religious Education in the Catholic school. This facilitated a general re-imagining of the aims and purposes of Religious Education in the Catholic school. It is important to state that this was not an *ex nihilo* creation of new subject parameters for Religious Education. It had come about as the wider Catholic academic community had sought to marry what was regarded as the best of the Smartian approach while retaining a necessary attachment—albeit rather faint at times—to Catholic principles. For example, the Catholic Bishops' Conference of England and Wales in 1986 issued a document on Religious Education which was informed heavily by the liberal philosophies of Religious Education current at that time.[42] This document explicitly questioned the role of Religious Education in faith formation and encouraged an approach which had more in common with a liberal 'Religious Studies' approach than with traditional catechesis. In contrast, the *Religious Education Curriculum Directory for England and Wales*, published in 2012, recognised both the challenges and possibilities offered by a more nuanced relationship between catechesis and Catholic Religious Education as proposed by the Magisterium.[43] This latter document is a welcome addition to the literature on this aspect of the Church's catechetical and educational mission.[44]

A key figure in the conceptual re-alignment between catechesis and Religious Education was Graeme Rossiter.[45] He pioneered the phrase 'creative divorce' to describe what he saw as a necessary separation between the subject of Religious Education in the Catholic school and wider catechetical processes. For Rossiter, such a 'creative divorce' would allow for an improvement in both catechesis and Religious Education and lead to a more integrated religious formation for young Catholics. Of course, a Catholic would always seriously question how any 'divorce' could be termed a creative as opposed to a destructive event. The serious point raised by Rossiter was that the school has a valuable role to play in the faith-life of the young person but, crucially, the catechetical mission of the school is not, and should not be, wholly contained within the Religious Education syllabus.

Rossiter would have been aware of the rapid developments in Church teaching on catechesis. While the Magisterium took an initially cautious approach to fostering reform in education, its approach to developments in catechesis was more urgent. The *General Directory for Catechesis*, published in 1997, developed themes emergent from its predecessor document, the *General Catechetical Directory* (from 1971) and the post-Synodal Exhortation of John Paul II, *Catechesi tradendae*, which appeared in 1979.[46] The *General Directory for Catechesis* dealt at length with all the *loci* and contexts of catechesis, including catechesis in schools, and reinforced the complementarity of the relationship between catechesis and school-based Religious Education which earlier documents on education had proposed.[47]

The charting of the development of catechesis and Religious Education understood as separate yet related components of religious formation is vital for a nuanced understanding of the contested nature of Catholic Religious Education today. Returning to the key questions of precedence (see above) it seems that catechesis, rightly, has precedence. The US Bishops' document *Doctrinal Elements of a Curricular Framework for the Development of Catechetical Materials for Young People of High School Age* is a case in point.[48] Its use of 'catechetical materials' in the title is significant as an indicator of the precedence of catechesis as a term rooted in the Church's ancient traditions. This substantial document sets out a range of doctrinal themes and accepts that their implementation depends on the context in which they are used. While this arrangement seems, on an initial reading at least, to run counter to the *General Directory for Catechesis*'s desire for some form of separation between catechesis and Religious Education, it offers a suitable *via media* which allows school-based educators to draw on the Church's doctrinal resources with a view to constructing orthodox and challenging programmes of Religious Education in the Catholic school.

Overall, it seems that the challenge for Catholic educators and school leaders is to navigate the complex common ground which catechesis and Catholic Religious Education share. To do so successfully needs firm grounding in the academic terrain and a broad and deep understanding of the development of Magisterial teaching in this area. A balanced and faithful adherence to this task will enrich discussions of how to enhance the school's wider mission.

Opponents of Catholic schooling and 'religious' schools in general point out that the provision of specific faith formation should properly lie outwith the life of the school. Education, in this line of thinking, is concerned with the formation of the mind and governed by what, to the Catholic mind, is a truncated understanding of the faculty of reason. Furthermore, it needs to be recognised that the Catholic school cannot operate a default setting which is inimically hostile to broader developments in education and curricular theory. Indeed an academically and doctrinally well-formed Catholic teacher will appreciate the benefits which can accrue to schools from engaging with genuine advances in understanding of educational theories. The area of contention is where fashionable educational ideas seem to cut across themes which are central to the Catholic vision of education.

By way of summation, Catholic education and schooling is a key element in the culture of pluralism. It seeks to offer its insights to the wider educational community. Indeed, the Catholic school should proclaim its public role which is underpinned by its specific 'ecclesial identity' and associated theological and anthropological vision. It is this unique blend of the public and the private which affords Catholic education a valued place in the public square.

Concluding Remarks

This chapter has explored two key challenges to the life of the Catholic school today. It does not claim to be an exhaustive treatment of the contemporary situation but the selected examples remind all Catholic educators of the challenges which the Catholic school has to address.

The questions arising from the 'ecclesial identity' of the Catholic school challenge the very foundations of the Catholic school. There is always a risk in opening debate on the relationship between the Church and the Catholic school as some would argue that any reimaging of the traditionally close relationship is a concession to secularism. This is a serious charge but, in actual fact, the opposite is true. To ensure that the Catholic school offers an alternative view of education the school must continually reflect on how it discharges its duties and fulfils its wider responsibilities. This openness to dialogue is the sign of a confidence in the Truth of the Gospel.

Regarding the curricular subject of Catholic Religious Education, similar principles apply. In proposing that Catholic Religious Education be separate but related to catechesis, the Church acknowledges the changing face of the Catholic school and seeks to use Catholic Religious Education to propose Jesus Christ the *Via Veritas Vita* for all people. It is right that the contours of any curricular subject should evolve in response to wider research-informed developments. The Catholic school does not sit on the sidelines of educational developments as if it were a disinterested observer. Indeed history shows that it is the Catholic Church in its mission to education which has often effected substantial reforms in educational practices.

Looking ahead, there remains a considerable challenge in articulating what is actually understood by the Catholic educational tradition in a contemporary academic environment so often influenced and shaped, as we know, by philosophies of education which do not accord with the Catholic worldview. Perhaps this challenge is most acute in the programmes of study, whether college or university-based, for the education of future Catholic teachers. Of course, teacher education programmes have often fallen victim to the less than nuanced 'anti-transmission' ideologies which came to prominence in the 1960s and which retain a considerable following among a wide range of educationalists today. Furthermore, it is not unfair to say that most Catholic school teachers are unaware that they are the inheritors of a tradition whose luminaries includes such influential historical figures as St Augustine of Hippo, St John Baptiste de la Salle and Josef Jungmann. It is hence incumbent upon all Catholic teacher educators to draw on the Church's extensive educational resources in order to continue and develop this tradition for present and future generations. In so doing, the authentic Catholic educator will be animated by a hope which plans for success, not failure. He or she will continually seek opportunities to effect reform in practice and, in union with the living Magisterium of the Church, will invite all to dialogue with the insights of the Catholic educational tradition.

Notes

1 H. Arendt, 'The Crisis in Education' in *Between Past and Future Six Exercises in Political Thought* (Middlesex: Penguin Books, 1954:2006), pp. 170–193.

2 C. Dawson, *The Crisis in Western Education* (New York: Sheed and Ward, 1961 / Washington D.C.: Catholic University of America Press, 2010).

3 G. Grace and J. O'Keefe SJ, 'Catholic Schools Facing the Challenges of the 21st Century' in G. Grace and J. O'Keefe SJ (Eds.) *International Handbook of Catholic Education* (Dordrecht / Boston: Springer, 2007), pp. 1–11.

4 A very helpful and concise overview of the key issues is found in F. Ouellet, 'Religious Education and Citizenship in Post-Modern Societies' in M. de Souza et al. (Eds.), *International Handbook of the Religious, Moral and Spiritual Dimensions in Education: Part One* (Dordrecht / Boston: Springer, 2006), pp. 363–374.

5 J. Arthur, L. Gearon and A. Sears *Education, Politics and Religion: Reconciling the Civil and the Sacred in Education* (London: Routledge Falmer, 2010), p. 18.

6 B. Carmody, 'Towards a Contemporary Catholic Philosophy of Education' in *International Studies in Catholic Education* 3/2 (2011) pp. 106–119.

7 'The complexity of the modern world makes it all the more necessary to increase awareness of the ecclesial identity of the Catholic school. It is from its Catholic identity that the school derives its original characteristics and its "structure" as a genuine instrument of the Church, a place of real and specific pastoral ministry' (*The Catholic School on the Threshold of the Third Millennium* 11).

8 J. Ratzinger/Pope Benedict XVI, *Pilgrim Fellowship of Faith: The Church as Communion* (San Francisco: Ignatius Press, 2005); Congregation for the Doctrine of the Faith, *Letter to the Bishops of the Catholic Church on Some Aspects of the Church Understood as Communion* (1992).

9 *The Catholic School on the Threshold of the Third Millennium* (1997), 11; *The Religious Dimension of Education in a Catholic School* (1988), 44.

10 Congregation for Catholic Education, *Lay Catholics in Schools Witnesses to Faith* (1982), 41; *The Catholic School* (1977), 34.

11 *Lay Catholics in School: Witnesses to Faith* (1982); *The Religious Dimension of Education in a Catholic School* (1988).

12 The leadership and commitment of the Head Teacher (School Principal) is key to the establishment of a solid Catholic ethos in a school. See, for example, N. Walbank, 'What Makes a School Catholic?' in *British Journal of Religious Education* vol. 34/ 2 (March 2012), pp. 169–180.

13 Professor Gerald Grace has used the term 'spiritual capital' to describe the array of faith-based traditions and practices which underpin the life of the Catholic school. See G. Grace, *Catholic Schools: Mission, Markets, Morality* (London: Routledge Falmer, 2002).

14 See, for example, Pope Benedict XVI, *Ubicumque et Semper* (2010): 'The Second Vatican Council already included among its central topics the question of the relationship between the Church and the modern world. In view of this conciliar teaching, my Predecessors reflected further on the need to find adequate ways to help the people of our time to hear the living and eternal Word of the Lord.'

15 For a more detailed examination of the place of the 'new evangelisation' in Catholic schools, see R. Rymarz, *The New Evangelisation: Issues and Challenges for Catholic Schools* (Ballan VIC: Connor Court Publishing, 2012).

16 John Sullivan and James Arthur offer illustrative examples of the differing Catholic perspectives on the 'inclusivity' or otherwise, of the Catholic school. Cf: J. Arthur, *The Ebbing Tide Policy and Principles of Catholic Education* (Leominster: Gracewing, 1995); J. Sullivan, *Catholic Education Distinctive and Inclusive* (London: Kluwer Academic Publishers, 2001).

17 Pope Benedict XVI, *Address to Bishops of the United States of America*

(Regions X–XIII) on the 'Ad Limina' Visit (5 May 2012).

18 Synod of Bishops, *Instrumentum Laboris for the Synod on the New Evangelisation* (2012), 149, 151, 152.

19 Pope Benedict XVI, *Letter to the Romans on Education* (2008); *Address to the Diocesan Convention of the Rome* (2007).

20 Pope John Paul II, *Laborem exercens* (1981); Vatican II, *Apostolicam actuositatem*, 4, 13.

21 See, for example, the Encyclical of Pope Pius X *Acerbo nimis* (1905): 'In order to enkindle the zeal of the ministers of God, We again insist on the need to reach the ever-increasing numbers of those who know nothing at all of religion, or who possess at most only such knowledge of God and Christian truths as befits idolaters. How many there are, alas, not only among the young, but among adults and those advanced in years, who know nothing of the chief mysteries of faith; who on hearing the name of Christ can only ask? "Who is he. . . that I may believe in him?"'

22 Pope Benedict XVI, *Letter to the Romans on Education* (2008).

23 A fine anthology of classic texts on educational philosophy has been provided by R. Gamble (Ed.), *The Great Tradition: Classic Readings on What It Means to be an Educated Human Being* (Delaware: ISI Books, 2007).

24 S. Caldecott, *Beauty in the Word: Re-thinking the Foundations of Education* (Tacoma: Angelico Press, 2012).

25 See M. Morey, 'Education in a Catholic Framework' in J. Piderit SJ and M. Morey (Eds.), *Teaching the Tradition: Catholic Themes in Academic Disciplines* (Oxford: Oxford University Press, 2012).

26 The roots of this important theme are explored in J. Bowen, *A History of Western Education (Volume 3): The Modern West* (London: Methuen Ltd., 1981), pp. 545–550. Bowen's trilogy is a mine of essential information on the history of educational ideas with due recognition given to the contribution of Christianity to educational thought.

27 Drawing on the social teaching of the Church, *Gaudium et spes* reinforced the duty of Catholics to participate actively in public affairs.

28 Caldecott, *Beauty in the Word,* (2012).

29 T. Rausch SJ, 'Catholic Anthropology' in J. Piderit SJ and M. Morey (Eds.), *Teaching the Tradition: Catholic Themes in Academic Disciplines* pp. 31–45.

30 A. Wright, *Critical Religious Education, Multiculturalism and the Pursuit of Truth* (Cardiff: University of Wales Press, 2007), p. 3.

31 N. Smart, *The Phenomenon of Religion* (London/Oxford: Mowbrays, 1973); P. Barnes, 'The Contribution of Professor Ninian Smart to Religious Education' in *Religion*, vol. 31 (2001) pp. 317–319; K. O'Grady, 'Professor Ninian Smart, Phenomenology and Religious Education' in *British Journal of Religious Education* vol. 27/3 (2005),

pp. 227–237.

32 G. Moran, 'The Intersection of Religion and Religious Education' in *Religious Education* vol. 69/5 (1974) pp. 531–541; G. Rummery, *Catechesis and Religious Education in a Pluralist Society* (Sydney: EJ Dwyer, 1975).

33 T. Groome, *Christian Religious Education—Sharing Our Story and Vision* (San Francisco: Harper and Row, 1980); G. Rossiter, 'The Need for a Creative Divorce between Catechesis and Religious Education in Catholic Schools' in *Religious Education* vol. 77/1 (1982) pp. 21–40.

34 The academic literature on this topic is substantial. See, for example: L. Franchi, 'Catechesis and Religious Education: A Case-Study from Scotland' in *Religious Education* vol. 108/5 (2013) pp. 467–481; R. Rymarz, 'Catechesis and Religious Education in Canadian Catholic Schools' in *Religious Education* vol. 106/5 (2011), pp. 537–549; L. Franchi, 'St. Augustine, Catechesis and Religious Education' in *Religious Education* vol. 106/3 (2011), pp. 299–311; Wright, *Critical Religious Education, Multiculturalism and the Pursuit of Truth,* (2007); T. Groome, 'Total Catechesis/Religious Education A Vision for Now and Always' in: T. Groome and H. Horell, (Eds) *Horizons and Hopes The Future of Religious Education* (New Jersey: Paulist Press, 2003); Rossiter, The Need for a Creative Divorce between Catechesis and Religious Education in Catholic Schools' (1982); Moran, 'The Intersection of Religion and Religious Education' (1974).

35 Congregation for Catholic Education, *Circular Letter to the Presidents of Bishops' Conferences on Religious Education in Schools* (2009).

36 *Ibid.* 17.

37 *Gravissimum educationis* was followed by a succession of partner documents: see footnote 39.

38 Pope Pius XI, *Divini illius magistri* (1929).

39 Congregation for Catholic Education, *The Catholic School* (1977); *Lay Catholics in Schools* (1982); *The Religious Dimension of Education in a Catholic School* (1988).

40 *The Religious Dimension of Education in a Catholic School* (1988), 67.

41 An important angle to this debate is the lack of consistency in the translation of 'religious education' into other languages. In Italian, for example, terms like *educazione religiosa, formazione religiosa* and *istruzione religiosa* are used interchangeably for the English subject title of 'religious education'.

42 J. Gallagher, *Living and Sharing Our Faith-National Project of Catechesis and Religious Education* (London: Collins Liturgical Publications, 1986).

43 *Catholic Bishops' Conference of England and Wales: Department of Catholic Education and Formation, Religious Education Curriculum Directory for England and Wales (2012).*

44 Cf: Franchi, 'Catechesis and Religious Education: A Case-Study from

Scotland' (2013); Rymarz, 'Catechesis and Religious Education in Canadian Catholic Schools' (2011).

45 Rossiter, 'The Need for a Creative Divorce between Catechesis and Religious Education in Catholic Schools' (1982).

46 Congregation for the Clergy, *General Directory for Catechesis* (1997); *General Catechetical Directory* (1971); Pope John Paul II, *Catechesi tradendae*, (1979).

47 'The relationship between religious instruction (sic) in schools and catechesis is one of distinction and complementarity: "there is an absolute necessity to distinguish clearly between religious instruction and catechesis"' (*General Directory for Catechesis*, 73).

48 United States Conference of Catholic Bishops, *Doctrinal Elements of a Curricular Framework for the Development of Catechetical Materials for Young People of High School Age* (2008).

2

EDUCATION AS CULTURAL RENEWAL

IN 1985, AT the dedication of a statue of Paul VI in Brescia Cathedral, Cardinal Agostino Casaroli was eloquence itself in his summation of the significance of the pontificate of one so committed to dialogue with the modern world. 'The story of human progress,' he stated, 'is nothing other than the chronicle of results obtained by dialogue with other people, with the environment, with the people who have preceded us and, in a sense, with those who will come after us.'[1] What was particularly significant about the Cardinal's words is that he was saying something profoundly true not just of the value of dialogue as conversation between persons, institutions or, even, philosophical positions but also—perhaps more importantly—making a statement about the very definition of modern 'culture'.

Culture has a dialogic dynamic, thriving on relationships—positive and negative—between societal views of the beliefs and activities of human beings in the past and present with an eye to the future. Fergus Kerr encapsulates this fundamental insight in prefacing a work by Tracey Rowland: 'We are only ourselves in relation to others, yet in relation to others we are truly ourselves. We must be abroad for the sake of others if we are to be at home with ourselves.'[2] In this chapter we argue that if cultures are to renew themselves, then it is conversation which requires rejuvenation.[3] In the case of Catholic education, that will involve dialogue inside the Church as well as without. Ideally, conversations best benefit all parties where the skill to listen is as actively displayed as the ability to articulate a viewpoint. The consequent nuances of interpretation involved in such an assertion will be revisited during the course of the chapter.

Historical Antecedents

The idea that education might be an instrument of 'cultural renewal' is, of course, hardly a novel concept. In the late 1950s, Lawrence K. Frank delivered a prestigious lecture at Harvard University entitled *The School as Agent for Cultural Renewal* which sought in particular to establish a role for the arts and humanities in providing a more affective appreciation of culture as well as communicating enduring goals and values which characterise communities: educational agencies should be key actors in a process of cultural renewal.[4] The implication that the school (and other educational institutions) should be, effectively, the engine-room of renewal is resonant of the aspirations which have been placed on schools by society as a principal means of engineering desired cultural, social and economic outcomes, particularly in the modern age of compulsory attendance.[5]

However, Frank's admonitions had roots which can be discerned across centuries rather than decades. In broad terms, when viewed with a heavy dose of hindsight, the history of western civilisation has been punctuated by periods of cultural renewal driven forward by educational reform. The medieval centuries in particular offer striking examples. Part of the perceived glory of Charlemagne (742–814) lay in his patronage of the great English scholar Alcuin of York (d. 804) whose high expectations of his students drove a thirst for beauty of image and Latin text in an age still characterised by bloodfeud and violence. With the advent of universities in the twelfth and thirteenth centuries, emerging out of monastic and canonical centres of learning, scholars depicted themselves as 'dwarfs on the shoulders of giants', in deference to past masters.[6] However, in practice, men such as Peter Abelard (1079–1142) and Hugh of St Victor (1096–1141) laid foundations which would lead to the compendious achievements of a Thomas Aquinas

(1225–74) or Albertus Magnus (d. 1280) in synthesising a Christian response to 'new knowledge' mediated to the Latin West via translations from Arabic. Although superficially this was a world of the intellect largely inhabited by men, women were not, in fact, invisible, represented by the likes of Abelard's student Heloise (d. 1164) and Hildegard of Bingen (1098–1179), the latter recently declared a Doctor of the Church.

One could go on across the centuries and the globe. Suffice it to stress here that the past would seem to offer clear precedents for cultural change being driven by emerging educational practices and needs which themselves were responses to evolving social realities, e.g. the greater urban presence of Abelard's twelfth-century world being distinctive from Charlemagne's ninth-century landscape. However, there is always a danger with such arguments based on historical precedent that too precipitous a leap is made towards concluding that education might serve the *same* transformative purpose in changing the dominant culture of the twenty-first century. As ever in scholarship, some further exacting issues need to be addressed before somewhat tentative conclusions are proposed.

Changing a Culture?

Culture itself, to begin with, is a difficult concept to define.[7] In 2003, for example, Cardinal Giacomo Biffi, Archbishop of Bologna, identified three co-existing interpretations of culture: the cultivation of the human person; a collective system of evaluating ideas, actions and events; attributes specific to a people, including mentality, institutions and customs.[8] In this chapter, however, 'culture' is a shorthand for the complexity of habits, rituals, common frames of reference, ideas and concepts shared by communities and peoples in ways which may encapsulate common characteristics but not necessarily to the extent that they exclude others who may share in some of those habits. Culture can be a means of building bridges with others rather than creating introspective cliques (though, sadly, this latter can, indeed, be the case). Generosity of spirit should inform any culture which is vibrant and life-affirming. It is in this context that one appreciates the famous insight of Paul VI that the Church is, by definition, missionary, reaching out to the world.[9]

If defining culture is difficult, even more so perhaps is the business of awarding adjectives such as 'dead', 'flourishing', 'moribund', 'contemporary' and so on. Take Latin for example: while the study of this language may not be at the centre of modern educational systems in the way that it once was in past centuries, it is hard not to find the fingerprints of a Latin culture—and, let it not be overlooked, of the Greek which pre-dated it—in territories once ruled by imperial Rome and, indeed, by way of the migrations of countless immigrants, the spread of such influences to 'new worlds' unknown to the ancients of Europe. The ideas of philosophers, the categorisation of the physical world, the roots of vernacular languages: all of these, in a way, mean that there is a little of the Greek or Roman in so many of us. Is it accurate, therefore, to describe Latin as a 'dead language' and the culture it supported for so many centuries best left to the attentions of antiquarians and historians? Is this the 'grand narrative' of decline one must accept despite the intimations of survival alluded to above?

Yet it is contemplation of the attempted revival of a classical Latin culture in the 15th century which can draw us towards a greater understanding of the issue as to whether a culture can ever renew itself.[10] The Renaissance—literally the period so-called of 're-birth'—may on the one hand have promoted more accurate texts on which many scholars lavished hours of study but the insistence on 'the style of Cicero' as archetype of Latinate expression had huge implications for stylistic forms which had continued to develop over the centuries of the Middle Ages.[11] No matter how attractive periods in the past might be—with their notable painters, sculptors, historians and poets—it is hard to swallow sometimes that what is past is past, never to be completely recaptured. This is an important historical insight when looking more closely at renewal in an ecclesial context.

Catholic Intellectual Tradition

Moving from the generic to the more specific, however, what is meant by the term 'Catholic culture'? Another term often seen nowadays is 'Catholic intellectual tradition': is this, in fact, a synonym of 'Catholic culture'?[12] The distinguished Jesuit scholar, Gerald A. McCool, addressed something of the same questions in his search for what he termed 'the Catholic mind.'[13] That 'mind' is not so much a philosophical construct as an attempt to encapsulate an approach to reality which is integrated in its use of the liberal arts, the sciences, and theology in understanding what is important and, perhaps controversially, 'the best' in human experience. In the second decade of the twenty-first century, there is a charge to be met that we do not have the confidence of our co-religionists of a hundred years ago in making serious claims for the existence of such a thing as 'the Catholic mind'. Why is this the case and why is the advocacy of a 'Catholic intellectual tradition' in danger of becoming an exclusive distinguishing mark of particular schools of thought or movements rather than a mantra of the Catholic educational mission *per se*?[14]

The first issue in the search for a 'Catholic intellectual tradition' must be that the debate in the Anglophone world has been too eager perhaps to emphasise the downside of such a concept. Part of the reason for this, of course, lies in the religious history of the British Isles, prevalent with the counter-narratives of Protestant and Catholic—narratives which migrated to the 'new worlds' of the Americas, Australia and New Zealand. This is partly the reason why postmodernism has struggled, to a degree, to have the impact it might otherwise have had for there is not one *grand narrative* but two, running parallel to each other, vying for legitimacy. For Catholics since the Reformation, many of the principal heroes of the narrative have been converts of whom the greatest (certainly the most famous) was John Henry Newman, made a cardinal early in the pontificate of Leo XIII (1878-1903). Newman, as McCool amply demonstrates, was one who sought above all to stress the integrated nature of knowledge, viewed through the eyes of a living faith, which brought particular insight and cohesion to one's understanding of the world, past, present and future.

For Newman, a classicist steeped in the study of the early Fathers, conversion to Rome had emerged as a necessary step as he began to appreciate more and more the historical contexts through which theology had developed. A compelling logic propelled Newman eventually, in 1845, to 'cross the Tiber' in order to feel himself rooted once more in the city of catacombs and Simon Peter. However, Newman himself remained appreciative of his Anglican origins, understanding life not as merely the sum of various parts but a joined-up experience.[15] He knew the value of his own Oxford education. This is why he sought to set up a Catholic university in Ireland. While banned from any opportunity to graduate from British universities, including Oxbridge, Newman was keen for Catholics to have the option of studying the humanities in order to be all the better informed in articulating Catholic perspectives. What Newman set out in *The Idea of the University* was visionary but it needs to be read mindful of the fact that it is the work of the author of the *Apologia pro vita sua*—a text which has its historical precursor in Augustine's *Confessions*. In short, Newman provides the scholar with a problem related to genre: is he writing deeply profound analysis of his contemporary scene or highly accomplished apologetic?[16] Herein lies the rub: for it could be argued that in seeking to promote a new appreciation of 'Catholic culture'—more specifically, the 'Catholic intellectual tradition'—one must avoid the temptation to narrow the canon of that culture to a lineage of which Newman is the lynchpin, and of which the likes of Hilaire Belloc, G K Chesterton and Christopher Dawson represent later manifestations. This is important for we really do need to be clear what we actually mean by 'Catholic culture' before we start to urge its recovery through education.

The problem with analyses of Catholic culture, therefore, is that they can be (a) too anglocentric (or, at the very least, eurocentric) and (b) precious about 'club membership'. Let us develop the first of these observations further before moving on to the second. There can be little doubt that turning one's eyes across the Atlantic from Europe towards the United States provides a glimpse of how Catholic higher education institutions have sought to rediscover and re-articulate for the twenty-first century the mission of Catholic education. This is a context (i.e. a richly diverse network of Catholic higher education institutions) largely unknown in the UK. Establishments ranging from the Catholic University of America in Washington DC to the University of Notre Dame (Indiana) and Sacred Heart University (Connecticut) have been beacons of the 'Catholic intellectual tradition' since their foundations. While the perceived 'catholicity' of some American Catholic universities and colleges has been put under the microscope in recent times, the looking afresh at what 'puts the Catholic in the Catholic college' should not be interpreted as mere reactive navel-gazing.[17] It is simply what needs to be done—indeed, John Paul II urged as much in *Ex corde ecclesiae*.[18] The writings of the Jesuit scholar, John Piderit, and Melanie Morey are typical of a genre which has emerged in America amongst Catholic educationalists who would seek to be hard-headed in their analyses of the current state of Catholic education.[19] This is post-apologetic—rather than postmodern—literature for it is rooted in the mindset and structures of rigorous, contemporary scholarship, seeking to articulate challenges but remaining, nonetheless, sanguine about Catholic education's future. Yet challenges there are, as James Heft's recent volume on Catholic high schools in

America has made clear.[20] Nevertheless, viewed from the UK, the American context provides a scenario where many similar problems may be present, including the fundamental realignment of Catholic education in response to changing demographics and the loss of a natural base of support due to increasing lapsation (especially amongst a younger age-group who represent the parents of the future), but at the same time there is a sense in which the mainstream American debate is not quite so starkly defined by the inherited dualism of the 'Old World' of the post-Reformation period and beyond. In short, American culture is just so varied—the debates so multi-faceted—that advocates of Catholic education should, ideally, be able to face the arguments of secularists in a conversation which does not seek to impose or pontificate but, rather, to engender respect for each other. That is the ideal if not always the reality. Secularist positions need to be listened to but respect needs to be reciprocal. Emerging out of a long tradition of Catholic scholarship, therefore—of which the Jesuit contribution merits particular mention—the history and continuing existence of Catholic higher education institutions in the United States provides a bedrock and sustaining context for civil dialogue and scholarly exchange amongst contested positions in discerning the cultural 'runes' of the contemporary age.

To turn to the second issue—who can 'join the club' as a fellow architect of Catholic culture in modern times?—one must first clear the air. If readers have already formed the impression that the argument being developed here would seek to play down the contribution of Newman, Belloc, Chesterton, Dawson et al., they would be wrong. Rather, what is required is some critical distance, approaching this 'English Catholic intellectual community' (to borrow Lothian's phrase[21]) with the aim of assessing their achievements against the wider contexts of the cultural and intellectual movements of their time. It is the brief of the scholar to ask questions which probe time-honoured opinion. Part of this process must be for every generation to re-visit and re-assess the originality and incisiveness of the minds of the 'heroes' of the modern Catholic intellectual tradition in comparison with other leading thinkers of their day. Representative of a time when the numbers of Catholics attending universities in Britain ranged from insignificant to a small (unrepresentative perhaps) minority, it cannot surprise the interested observer that the role of educated adult converts to the Catholic faith has had a disproportionate impact in terms of influencing perceptions of a particular period in Catholic Anglophone history. In analysing the contribution of the 'great names', therefore, it is imperative that some middle-ground be found: whether evoking a 'golden age' of Catholic intellectual life or pointedly critiquing the concentrated focus on such writers' contributions, scholars should not be distracted from the real, lived cultural experience of the broader Catholic community in what was, for decades (certainly in a UK context), a predominantly working- and lower-middle-class Church.[22]

Beyond the Anglophone world, it is true, there are long-established pontifical higher education establishments elsewhere in Europe—in Leuven, Paris and Salamanca, not to mention Rome itself, for example. It is beyond the remit of this chapter to review the contributions of such pontifical institutions to any perceived Catholic intellectual tradition. Just one of many possible lines of research is how the works pre-eminently of Etienne Gilson and Jacques Maritain acted as conduits of French ideas about culture and society amongst a certain Catholic élite in Britain in the middle years of the twentieth century. Representative of a continental approach to philosophy, in contrast to the favoured analytical philosophy in Britain, the question still needs to be asked seriously whether such writers had any lasting impact in the Catholic community beyond the 'groves of academe' and self-motivated advocates. Part of the challenge here is that so much of the picture which emerges about the life of actual parish communities is built up from random anecdotes or highly localised studies which lack the rigour, depth and coherence, perhaps, of a longitudinal qualitative study. One thinks, in a UK context, of Jonathan Rose's *The Intellectual Life of the British Working Classes* as a signpost towards a possible way ahead—a Catholic equivalent is required in order to assess the extent of readership and impact of, for example, pamphlets of the Catholic Truth Society (founded 1868 and re-established in 1884) and other similar initiatives throughout the Anglophone world.[23]

The key argument here, therefore, is that the picture of the 'Catholic past' which scholarship has painstakingly built up in recent years is still a jigsaw with pieces missing. Sustained energies still require to be directed towards identified gaps in our knowledge and understanding of the lives of Catholic communities over past decades.[24] Consequently, one's present understanding of a 'Catholic intellectual tradition' must necessarily be fluid, remaining open to refinement as the fruits of further research become available. Nevertheless, it can be asserted with some confidence that any understanding of the Catholic intellectual tradition must be inhabited by a sense of looking forward as well as back to some 'golden age'.[25] Both John Paul II and Benedict XVI have promoted a spirit of hope for the future by way of a cultural renewal which contributes, more generally, to recognition of the key role of Christianity in forging Western societies—or, at the very least, the promotion of a civic culture which rejects knee-jerk antipathy towards Christianity in the public sphere.[26] From a Catholic perspective, this is a laudable and worthwhile aim but there remains a nagging fear that it may be unrealistic, given that the Christian voice in the West can be perceived to be on the retreat and to be 'on the retreat' is to be a non-player at the table of high-level decision-making and influence amongst national and global institutions.[27] Yet, as this chapter has tried to argue, renewal cannot mean another kind of retreat—this time self-imposed—to a nostalgic 'golden age' in the past. Whatever the future is going to bring for initiatives such as the 'Courtyard of the Gentiles', it must surely *not* result in the emergence of a new Gnosticism, i.e. the impression that the 'pure' faith is the property of an increasingly small number of strict adherents. The Church has fought the fight against such exclusivity throughout its history and Christ's mandate remains the same: to reach out to all.[28]

It is precisely in response to this scriptural proscription that Catholic education must ideally be seen to act in its encounters with children, young people and adults. In responding to the 'joys and sorrows' of the diverse range of learners in their schools and universities, Catholic teachers have an opportunity to be at the front-line of evangelisation. However, getting the balance right in accepting the challenges of being a Catholic educator remains a perennial task. Ultimately, the need to encourage creativity in young learners, along with independence of (critical) thought and initiative, *is* as important in the Catholic school as in its non-denominational counterpart. Yet, as the blogosphere quickly illustrates, there is an expectation abroad that these same schools project an identity which is firmly Catholic, characterised in terms of fidelity to the Magisterium.[29] Can the square be circled? This is the question which runs implicitly through the next section.

Education as Cultural Renewal

As already observed above, what is past is past. Perhaps the best that can be said is that cultures evolve anew with echoes of past eras.[30] Nevertheless, the term 'cultural renewal' is a convenient shorthand for a rediscovery of roots and customs which aid individuals and communities in their daily living. As sentient, rational and spiritual beings, we make choices about which aspects of past practice and thought we might wish to take ownership of again. Fundamentally, it is in the *choosing* of the emphases in such choices that critical engagement with any perceived 'tradition' passed down over centuries must be located. As Richard Liddy has so eloquently put it: 'the point of any authentic tradition is to change us in the present so that we can articulate the authentic meanings of the tradition into the future.'[31] In other words, tradition ought not to be viewed as an increasingly heavier *dead* weight on the shoulders of each successive generation but, rather, should be a liberating force which informs and enlightens people of the present in looking to the future.

What this means in real terms, of course, is not so easy to articulate. Other scholars' insights are useful here. John Haughey's pithy statement that 'there is a tradition that is in a continuum with the best of the past, and its openness to the best of the present is crucial for the future of human well-being' is apt and to-the-point.[32] Tradition is not a concrete block dragging one back to the past; rather it is an animating jet stream propelling one into the future. Respect for tradition does not denote nostalgic looking back to a perceived golden age but should provide a basis for constant aspiration towards the achievement of a golden age in the future. This is a fundamental mark of Christian hope—so often the forgotten virtue. Each successive generation of the Catholic family must take responsibility in passing on to its young people not only a content of faith and an example of charitable practice but also a spirit of Christian hope which does not baulk in the face of the multiple and complex challenges of present times and the near future.[33]

However, in constantly seeking that 'better day', the temptation to retreat into a theatre of existence occupied only by others of like-mind is a recipe, arguably, for disaster. If the proud confidence of the Gnostic is to be rejected in authentic Catholic culture, so too is an unsustainable puritanism. Medieval Cathars, for example, were condemned by the Church partly because of an idealised morality founded on a dualist rejection of the material world. With his eulogy of 'Brother Sun and Sister Moon' and celebration of the animals and birds which shared his world, the Cathars' contemporary, St Francis of Assisi (1181-1226), reminds us that the Catholic Church throughout the ages has predominantly rejoiced in God's material creation. So it is for us today: the challenge for the 21st century Catholic is to heal inherited rifts and enter into dialogue with fellow human beings of all faiths and none, especially where that dialogue is perceived to be faltering or, in some cases, non-existent, by way of building bridges. John Paul II reached out in charity during his seminal meetings with representatives of other faiths at Assisi, the town of St Francis; Benedict XVI offered a similar model, particularly during his foreign trips and exemplified most eloquently, perhaps, by his meeting with Muslim leaders in the Blue Mosque in Istanbul in 2006.[34]

However, notwithstanding what is asserted above about tradition and the choices people and communities make in living in the present and moving into the future, there is little doubt that the possession of an informed intellect, in tandem with a sympathetic disposition, is a key element in developing a deeper understanding of the world from a Catholic perspective. In other words, the Catholic should expect to be directed in the development of mental (as well as spiritual) tools to discern what is the right thing to do or say in living out the human experience. Melanie Morey puts it succinctly: 'the Catholic view of freedom [is a] positive freedom to do as we ought to do', adding perceptibly elsewhere that people need to learn to engage with the 'collective wisdom of past centuries and apply it critically in their current circumstances.'[35] Morey's insights—and in these she can rightly claim a long pedigree in both Catholic scholarship and pastoral documents—are meant to challenge the educator. It would be wrong to interpret the reference to critical encounter with ideas as in some way promoting elitism—a goal only achievable by the gifted few. Nor are such insights meant to be esoteric—fine words but not really relevant to people in the real world of brokenness, struggle and pluralist social realities. As has already been argued, Catholic culture cannot be about withdrawal from the world or a failure to view the world—

in all its rich variety—as it is. Rather, it is about demonstrating awareness: awareness of a heritage of ideas—founded on the salvific actions of a divine person, Jesus Christ—which has considered the 'big issues' of the centuries and which still has relevance for our contemporary situation. Catholic education—at school, university or college—offers, therefore, a special opportunity to invite young and older learners to go forward in harmony with a Catholic tradition clothed in the vibrant, generously eirenic guise promoted in this chapter.

In pursuance of this goal, it would seem obvious to begin with the formation of Catholic teachers themselves. While it is impossible to generalise about teacher education methodologies throughout the world, it can nevertheless be argued here that an enrichment of the process of preparation for the classroom might be achieved through a re-developed, core-curricular encounter with a specifically Catholic philosophy of education. This is not an argument for an ahistorical or exclusive engagement with certain ideas—in many ways that would be a pointless exercise (and, indeed, one could hardly claim even a modicum of expertise in any school of philosophy without awareness of the arguments of other contemporaries). It is, however, about entitlement—a case of providing Catholic student teachers with a gateway to a culture and worldview which, to the extent that they already identify themselves as members of the Church, they might already be perceived to share by association (particularly by sections of the mass media) but with which, in fact, they are largely unfamiliar in terms of their individual intellectual and spiritual development.[36] In this sense more broadly, Catholic education fulfils a fundamental role in preparing young people and others for the choices all human beings have to make in life. It is not, in the final analysis, about enforcing those decisions by diktat or attempting to exert thought-control (something properly antipathetic to the Christian message, particularly as articulated at the Second Vatican Council) but it is about unpatronisingly providing as many people as possible with a patiently constructed framework of theological, philosophical, moral and spiritual principles against which to make those decisions.

To declare, however, that Catholic education must provide a clearly demarcated *modus operandi* in comparison with the pronounced pragmatism of others—provision of an education which is best rather than useful—is to enter highly contentious waters. This is because any scholar tempted to navigate in the direction of this argument must be sure of his or her ground. Reduction of the educational principles and activities of others to pastiche is certainly to be avoided. There are few schools or universities, for example, which set out to make their students' lives worse off while many encourage charitable giving and community service. A *raison d'être* for a Catholic presence in the educational field, therefore, ought not to be predicated as a first principle on a negative comparison with other sectors as if what the Catholic school or educational establishment offered was quantifiably better. For a start, there is a sin of pride to contend with—traditionally one of the seven deadliest.

The advocacy of Catholic education must, therefore, begin 'at home' with an internal examination of conscience: is Catholic education in its many guises fulfilling its potential in preparing its learners to be 'the salt of the earth'?[37] Salt can be bitter-tasted and the phrase encapsulates the call to be Christ-like in questioning the dominant social mores of the age. In terms of identification with the institution of the Church—particularly in the once verdant terrains of Western Europe, now pock-marked with neglected roadside shrines and empty village churches—there is a real challenge for Catholic educators of the future in deciphering the signs of the times and summoning sufficient will to respond to perceptions of a now endemic pattern of haemorrhage.[38] Such a trend has consequences: the Church is required to face in Europe and elsewhere in the so-called developed world a proactive challenge to its inhabiting of the public space at all.[39] Hence the importance of encouraging a re-engagement with a Catholic philosophy of education amongst school managers and other interested parties, including in a particular way those intending to teach in Catholic schools. If culture is to be genuinely transformed in the light of the Christian Gospel, it will require the contributions of individuals who have a knowledge-base and an understanding of how Catholic thinking has developed over the centuries, including in the last hundred years or so, but also in preceding eras. For the purposes of contextualising such an ambition and how it might be framed, a few key texts immediately suggest themselves: these texts should be cross-examined and critiqued, with differences in emphasis noted and accounted for in terms of basic principles, intended audience and ultimate goals.[40]

Education, therefore, has a role in helping learners to be unafraid of ideas and to develop skills of discernment which can encourage critical thought rather than infatuation with what might otherwise be termed the 'current' or the 'modern'. Catholic education should, ultimately, guide learners towards an appreciation of the balance between faith and reason which makes for an enhanced engagement with modernity.[41] However, such a rationale for its existence demands consistent focus and effort in its leadership and co-constructors (i.e. teachers and students) and—including for those at advanced levels of study—may be a recipe for a vicious circle of disappointments as reality fails to live up to aspirations. How, then, can a holistic vision of the human person (intellectual, physical and spiritual), properly aware of the respective, intertwining roles of faith and reason in building-up a worldview, be best communicated to the wider population? Perhaps part of an answer lies beyond appeal to abstract argument; sometimes it is the *exemplum* of a fellow human being's experience of living a life dedicated to the marriage between reason and faith which is the most enlightening. An outstanding example is a 2003 essay by Thomas R. Flynn, Professor of Philosophy at Emory University, in which he eloquently articulates his accommodation of both reason and faith in the course of a review of his scholarly life.[42] Catholic educators could do worse than to reflect on and attempt to replicate something of the dynamic of Flynn's experience, searching for the triggers in his account which might make for a greater commonality of such a life-affirming response to the intellectual challenges of today. It is true, of course, that Catholic education must respond to a gritty actuality of countless community circumstances and predilections—but it remains no bad thing, in terms of seeking up-lifting goals for the future in the face of obstinate reality, to aspire towards an education which truly supports and encourages critical engagement with the faith/reason question and with the Catholic intellectual tradition more generally.

Concluding Remarks

Returning, finally, to the previously highlighted virtue of 'hope', there would seem to be an imperative need to hope that contemporary initiatives might begin to mend some of the broken bridges between Catholicism and the increasingly secularist culture of our age.[43] The 'Year of Faith' and the dialogue characterised as 'The Courtyard of the Gentiles' present opportunities for re-engagement at various levels of society—university, school, parish and other groupings. The extent to which they will be considered successes will be a brief for future historians and commentators but it would be surprising if the relationships between Church and State, religion and secularism, were not to generate continued debate in the press and other organs of popular opinion. Such dialogue is to be welcomed as a means by which Catholic perspectives might continue to be communicated to a wider constituency, for considered reflection where there is sufficient goodwill. As alluded to at the outset of this chapter, Catholic educators are called to play their part in creating the conditions within which such dialogue might be conducted. Ultimately, education is not about systems but about people and, to paraphrase Cardinal Jorge Mario Bergoglio (now Pope Francis), the profoundest identity of a teacher lies in the testimony and witness to a way of being which projects recognition of the dignity of the learner.[44] The teacher draws self-esteem from an ideal of service. In short, if educators are to be charged with the heady aspiration of renewing culture, they must, nonetheless, never lose sight of the needs and rights of individual learners in the drive for any perceived wider societal benefit.

Notes

1 Quoted in P. Hebblethwaite, *Paul VI: The First Modern Pope* (New York: Paulist Press, 1993), p. 6.

2 T. Rowland, *Culture and the Thomist Tradition: After Vatican II* (London: Routledge, 2003). The quotation is from Fergus Kerr's foreword (p. xiii).

3 The argument that 'cultural tradition' is 'a kind of *conversational* partner' is a crucial insight in Chapter 8 of P. Hogan, *The New Significance of Learning: Imagination's Heartwork* (London: Routledge, 2010), especially p. 120.

4 L. K. Frank, *The School as Agent for Cultural Renewal* (Cambridge, Mass.: Harvard University Press, 1959), pp. 40–41. The summary of Frank's thesis is taken from C. Kridel, 'The Play Element in Culture and the Use of Festivals in the General Education Curriculum' in *Journal of General Education*, vol. 32/3 (1980) pp. 232–233.

5 For further contextualisation of this issue, see the arguments in B. Barker, 'Can schools change society?' in *Forum* vol. 53/1 (2011) pp. 163-172.

6 D. D. McGarry, *The 'Metalogicon' of John of Salisbury: A Twelfth-Century Defense of the Verbal and Logical Arts of the Trivium* (Berkeley: University of California Press, 1955) p. 167.

7 Though published in 1964, the musings of John Wilson on the challenges involved in such conceptual definition still deserve note: see J. Wilson, 'Education and Indoctrination' in T. H. B. Hollins, *Aims in Education: The Philosophic Approach* (Manchester: Manchester University Press, 1964) pp. 24–25.

8 G. Biffi, 'Catholic Culture for True Humanism' in *L'Osservatore Romano* (22 January 2003) p. 7.

9 On Pope Paul VI's vision of 'evangelisation' at the heart of the Church's mission and identity, see R. Rymarz, 'John Paul II and the

'New Evangelization': Origins and Meaning' in *Australian eJournal of Theology* vol. 15/1 (2010) pp. 9–14.

10 Although focussing ultimately on a twelfth-century context, Gerhart B. Ladner's impressively assembled arguments concerning the lack of consistency in using terminology such as 'renaissance' or 'renewal' in a range of historical sources are still the best introduction to this scholarly debate. See G. B. Ladner, 'Terms and Ideas of Renewal' in R. L. Benson and G. Constable, *Renaissance and Renewal in the Twelfth Century*, (Oxford: Clarendon Press, 1982) pp. 1–33.

11 B. Roest, 'Rhetoric of Innovation and Recourse to Tradition in Humanist Pedagogical Discourse' in S. Gersh and B. Roest (Eds), *Medieval and Renaissance Humanism: Rhetoric, Representation and Reform*, (Leiden: Brill, 2003) p. 137.

12 An excellent précis of what is meant by 'Catholic intellectual tradition' has been provided by Boston College. The text is available at: http://www.bc.edu/content/dam/files/top/church21/pdf/cit.pdf. See also J. Turner, 'Catholic Intellectual Traditions and Contemporary Scholarship' in *Catholic Education: A Journal of Enquiry and Practice* vol. 2/1 (1998) pp. 35–45.

13 G. A. McCool, 'Spirituality and Philosophy: the Ideal of the Catholic Mind' in *Sacred Heart University Review* vol. 10/1, (1989) pp. 26–43.

14 See S. J. McKinney and J. Sullivan (Eds), *Education in a Catholic Perspective* (Aldershot: Ashgate, 2013), p. 4.

15 Newman's recounting of his decision to give up the living of St Mary's, Littlemore, is testimony to the fact that he became sensitive to the pastoral implications for Anglican communicants burdened with a pastor who had serious doubts about his own place in their ecclesial community. See J.H. Newman, *Apologia pro vita sua* (London: Longman, 1864) p. 337.

16 Philip Gleason's incisive observations re Catholics' 'proprietary feeling' towards Newman are particularly apt in alerting Catholic scholars to the ramifications of wearing 'rose-tinted spectacles'; nevertheless, Gleason's own judicious efforts amply demonstrate that balanced and careful scholarship can still go on to underline Newman's lasting contribution to the Catholic higher education debate. See P. Gleason, 'Newman's *Idea* in the minds of American educators' in J. C. Linck and R. J. Kupke, *Building the Church in America* (Washington D.C.: Catholic University of America Press, 1999), pp. 113–139, especially p. 113.

17 See the stimulating discussions in W. C. Graham (Ed.), *Here Comes Everybody: Catholic Studies in American Higher Education*, (Lanham: University Press of America, 2009), particularly the editor's own contribution on 'Seven attitudes and approaches that make a college Catholic' (pp. 18–26).

18 Pope John Paul II, *Ex corde ecclesiae*, (1990).

19 M. M. Morey and J. J. Piderit, *Catholic Higher Education: A Culture in Crisis*, (New York: Oxford University Press, 2006). See, also, the contrasting perspectives in J. C. Haughey, *Where is knowing going? The horizons of the knowing subject*, (Washington, DC: Georgetown University Press, 2009), pp. 159–161. The now classic text which provides a broad sweep of historical context to the contested story of Catholic universities and colleges is P. Gleason, *Contending with Modernity: Catholic Higher Education in the Twentieth Century* (New York: Oxford University Press, 1995).

20 J. Heft, *Catholic High Schools: Facing the New Realities* (New York: Oxford University Press, 2011).

21 J. R. Lothian, *The Making and Unmaking of the English Catholic Intellectual Community 1910–1950* (Notre Dame: University of Notre Dame Press, 2009).

22 J. L. Heft offers a similar insight in 'Theology's Place in a Catholic University', in P. W. Carey and E. C. Muller (eds), *Theological Education in the Catholic Tradition: Contemporary Challenges* (New York: Crossroad, 1997), pp. 193–194.

23 J. Rose, *The Intellectual Life of the British Working Classes* (New Haven: Yale University Press, 2010; 2nd ed.).

24 Two excellent examples of modern studies which point a way forward in terms of methodology to be adopted in building up a picture of Catholic culture 'on the ground' (as it were) are B. P. Clarke, *Piety and Nationalism: Lay Voluntary Associations and the Creation of an Irish-Catholic Community in Toronto, 1850-1895* (Montreal & Kingston: McGill-Queen's University Press, 1993) and S. K. Kehoe, *Creating a Scottish Church: Catholicism, Gender and Ethnicity in Nineteenth-Century Scotland* (Manchester: Manchester University Press, 2010).

25 A further question—deserving of more detailed attention elsewhere—is the extent to which the revisionist treatments of a new generation of scholars are impacting on the timeworn narrative of the 'Catholic intellectual tradition' in the early 20th century. More penetrating analysis of texts is uncovering nuances of difference amongst the leading figures which dilutes the monolithic impression of Catholic intellectual endeavour in this period, i.e. throwing into relief disagreements *between* Catholic intellectuals rather than (or as well as) differences with secularists or apologists of other worldviews. An excellent introduction to this more sophisticated approach is S. Schloesser, 'The Rise of a Mystic Modernism: Maritain and the Sacrificed Generation of the Twenties' in R. Heynickx and J. De Maeyer (Eds.) *The Maritain Factor: Taking Religion into Interwar Modernism* (Leuven: Leuven University Press, 2010), pp. 29–39, especially p. 34 where a subtle distinction in Jacques Maritain's understanding of Thomistic hylomorphism is discussed in contrast

to others.

26 See, for example, Pope John Paul II, *Ecclesia in Europa* (2003).

27 However, note the more nuanced analysis of the waning influence of religion in the West in R. Audi, 'Natural Reason, Religious Conviction, and the Justification of Coercion in Democratic Societies', in L. Zucca and C. Ungureanu (Eds), *Law, State and Religion in the New Europe: Debates and Dilemmas* (Cambridge: Cambridge University Press, 2012), p. 91.

28 Mt 28:19.

29 A recent challenging prognosis of the tensions inherent here is to be found in G. P. McDonough, *Beyond Obedience and Abandonment* (Montreal & Kingston: McGill-Queen's University Press, 2012).

30 Two scholars who are particularly alive to the complexities of the cultural renewal debate are S. Nieto, 'Culture and Education' in D. L. Coulter and J. R. Wiens (Eds.), *Why do we educate? Renewing the conversation* (Malden: Blackwell, 2008), pp. 127–143, and J. Zimmermann, *Humanism and Religion: A Call for the Renewal of Western Culture* (New York: Oxford University Press, 2012).

31 R. M. Liddy, 'The Catholic Intellectual Tradition: Achievement and Challenge' in T. M. Landy (Ed.), *As Leaven in the World: Catholic Perspectives on Faith, Vocation and the Intellectual Life* (Franklin: Sheed & Ward, 2001), pp. 5–6.

32 Haughey, *Where is knowing going?* (2009), p. xii.

33 On hope as a forgotten virtue, see P. Kreeft, *Fundamentals of the Faith: Essays in Christian Apologetics*, (San Francisco: Ignatius Press, 1988), pp. 176–180.

34 V. Tirimanna, 'Pope Benedict's Prayer in the Blue Mosque' in *Studies in Interreligious Dialogue* vol. 18/1 (2008) pp. 29–45.

35 M. M. Morey, 'Education in a Catholic Framework' in Piderit and Morey (Eds.) *Teaching the Tradition: Catholic Themes in Academic Disciplines* (2012), pp. 411 and 399 respectively.

36 See, for example, R. Coll, 'Student teachers' perception of their role and responsibilities as Catholic educators' in *European Journal of Teacher Education* vol. 30/4 (2007) pp. 456–457.

37 Mt 5:13. Vatican II, *Lumen Gentium*, 33, uses the 'salt of the earth' image with particular reference to the laity.

38 S. J. Hunt, *Alternative Religions: A Sociological Introduction* (Aldershot: Ashgate, 2003), pp. 8, 232–236; J. L. Allen, *The Catholic Church: What Everyone Needs To Know* (New York: Oxford University Press, 2013), pp. 10–11.

39 U. Nowak, '"Wall of Separation?" Religion's Presence in the Public Sphere of a Democratic State—Some Theoretical Reflections', in I. Borowik and M. Zawita (Eds.), *Religions and Identities in Transition*, (Kraków: Nomos, 2010, pp. 119–130); P. Jenkins, *The New Anti-Catholicism: The Last Acceptable Prejudice* (New York: Oxford University Press,

2003) might profitably be read alongside the shorter article by J. Martin, "The Last Acceptable Prejudice" in *America: The National Catholic Weekly* (25 March 2000) available at http://www.americamagazine.org/content/article.cfm?article_id=606.

40 T. Corcoran, 'The Catholic Philosophy of Education' in *Studies: An Irish Quarterly Review* vol. 19, (1930) pp. 199–210; J. D. Redden and F. A. Ryan, *A Catholic Philosophy of Education* (Milwaukee: Bruce Publishing, 1942); J. L. Elias, 'Whatever Happened to Catholic Philosophy of Education?' in *Religious Education* vol. 94/1, (1999) pp. 92–109; E. A. Joseph, 'The Philosophy of Catholic Education' in T. C. Hunt, E. A. Joseph, and R. J. Nuzzi (Eds.), *Handbook of Research of Catholic Education* (Westport: Greenwood Press, 2001), pp. 27–63; C. L. Hancock, *Recovering a Catholic Philosophy of Elementary Education* (Mount Pocono: Newman House Press, 2006); B. Carmody, 'Towards a contemporary Catholic philosophy of education' (2011), pp. 106–119; S. Whittle, 'Towards a contemporary philosophy of Catholic Education: moving the debate forward', in *International Studies in Catholic Education* vol. 6/1 (2014) pp. 46–59.

41 S. E. Cuypers, 'The Ideal of a Catholic education in a secularized society' in *Catholic Education: A Journal of Inquiry and Practice* vol. 7/4 (2004) pp. 426–445, especially. p. 434.

42 T. R. Flynn, 'Athens and Jerusalem, Paris and Rome', in C. L. Hancock and B. Sweetman, *Faith and the Life of the Intellect* (Washington DC: The Catholic University of America Press, 2003), pp. 1–18.

43 An incisive summary of the historical roots of this breakdown in relations is to be found in H. McLeod, 'The Present Crisis in Historical Context' in L. Kenis, J. Billiet and P. Pasture (Eds.), *The Transformation of the Christian Churches in Western Europe 1945–2000* (Leuven: Leuven University Press, 2010) pp.23–38. McLeod is particularly succinct in his analysis of why the current 'crisis' is different from other apparent historical antecedents.

44 J. M. Bergoglio/Pope Francis and A. Skorka, *On Heaven and Earth* (Translated by A. Bermudez and H. Goodman) (London: Bloomsbury, 2013), p. 132. This book was originally published in Spanish in 1995.

3

MEDIA, EDUCATION AND CULTURE

In the summer of 2011, many English cities erupted in street battles. Cars were burned, shops were looted and gangs of young people ran riot through city centres. The outbreak of mob rule engendered a degree of soul searching among commentators, politicians and the general public. Various causes were suggested but one universally recognised ingredient of the spread of violence was the role of the media. Rolling news channels gave 24 hour-a-day attention to the disorder, newspapers screamed for emergency tactics to be employed and for the army to reclaim the streets. Most interesting perhaps (in the context of this study) was the role played by social media. That a key role was played is beyond doubt: analysing its impact is rather harder. While one police force denounced the use of Twitter, suggesting that it allowed co-ordinated miscreancy, other forces used exactly the same social networking platform to broadcast information to terrified residents, and appeal for calm! The presence of the media in such narratives is easy to expose and analyse. What is harder to define is the pervasive and potent presence of the media in other areas of society, including the educational world. In this chapter we show how the worlds of the media (new and otherwise) and education are necessary partners in support of the Catholic cultural project.

Possibilities Offered by New Media

The simplicity, cost-effectiveness and scope of the new media offer the Church a unique opportunity to propose its millennial teaching to a twenty-first century humanity hungry for wisdom, transcendence and challenge. This has been repeatedly recognised by the Popes of recent years, who have, on the one hand encouraged the use of new media as a tool of educational value, while at the same time warning of its potential for dehumanisation. As Pope Benedict XVI stated in the message for World Communications Sunday in 2011:

> New horizons are now open that were until recently unimaginable; they stir our wonder at the possibilities offered by these new media and, at the same time, urgently demand a serious reflection on the significance of communication in the digital age. This is particularly evident when we are confronted with the extraordinary potential of the Internet and the complexity of its uses. As with every other fruit of human ingenuity, the new communications technologies must be placed at the service of the integral good of the individual and of the whole of humanity. If used wisely, they can contribute to the satisfaction of the desire for meaning, truth and unity which remain the most profound aspirations of each human being.

A deeper reflection on Benedict's comments allows us to see where the influence of the media articulates with the world of education. It is a truism to state that there is a close relationship between education and communication. This relationship is based on the fact that we educate *by communicating*—an educational relationship uses words, gestures and actions but also artificial languages and channels of communication, everything from handwriting to modern digital technology. At the same time, we educate people *to communicate*: to read and write and count, but also to speak well, to use technology to transmit ideas. The relationship is both mutually enriching and essential.[1]

The capacity for communication is rooted in our nature, in our capacity to express meaning through language and other means, but it needs to be cultivated; it needs to be learnt through interaction with parents, teachers, friends and so on. However, more radically, both communication and education bear witness to man's need to be in 'relationship' to others: 'no man is an island', while being a well-known phrase is also a theologically potent statement. Pope Francis highlighted this in his first Communications Day Message:

> In a world like this, media can help us to feel closer to one another, creating a sense of the unity of the human family which can in turn inspire solidarity and serious efforts to ensure a more dignified life for all. Good communication helps us to grow closer, to know one another better, and ultimately, to grow in unity.[2]

Thus communication is the most natural and normal of human activities, the glue which holds our life together from the simplest social relationship to complicated institutional arrangements. Nowadays that glue is made up of more than words and sounds but also by text messages, Facebook postings and even the now ubiquitous 'selfies'. Seen from a theological perspective, this intuition goes to the very heart of the Christian faith.

Catholic educators need foundational grounding in the Church's theology of communication, or theology of relationship (grace), which articulates the theological principles for being Catholic in a digital culture-continent. A theology of the Trinity is the base upon which our theology of communication is built. The Trinity's inner life as self-communicating love reflects a dynamic and intimate sharing among persons. The technical term for this is *communio.* We are called to imitate this communication by allowing love to be the content and the process of our personal bonds with others.[3]

The Media of Communication

The authors of the best-selling book *La Sfida Educativa,* published by the Italian Episcopal Conference (CEI) distinguish three major types of educational community. The volume considers the role of the media in educating people of today to understand, create and foster community understood as a network of relationships between individuals and/or groups within society, based on the sharing of knowledge, information and attitudes.

The first community is made up of the means of communication such as telephone, mobiles, email, chatrooms, blogs, forums and what we would now call social networks - media which young people make ever greater use of in building relationships. These media allow users to enlarge and extend their *community of communication* with others by overcoming the limitations of space and time. They allow users to maintain and build on pre-existing relationships and to put them in touch with people with whom they would have no other way of communicating. Perhaps the best example of this is the @Pontifex twitter account with its almost five million English language followers.

It is clear, however, that such relationships are not merely leisure pursuits. They are genuine educational encounters. Users engage in a form of peer education which is, potentially, more powerful today than traditional magisterial forms of teaching. For the Catholic educator, the emergence of a new competitor for the engagement of students, a competitor who is always present in the life of the student, who requires little in the way of effort, who allows the student to delete, omit or otherwise ignore unpalatable truths, represents a profoundly serious challenge. Understanding the implications of this may require decades of reflection. However the *educational emergency* of which Benedict XVI and Francis speak allows no such luxury.[4] It is imperative that Christian educators respond positively now to the reality in which they find themselves.

This reality is very different from the second, more traditional territorially-based educational community made up of concrete links (family or neighbourhood or school). Here the Catholic educator is on what might be defined "home territory". But here too the method of delivery of the message must be considered against a backdrop of changing social customs—a particular problem is the ever-greater tendency (facilitated by such technological innovations as the TV remote control, the fast-forward button and the plethora of entertainment choices) to 'switch off' if content is delivered in a 'non-entertaining' manner. While the tendency to showmanship and gimmickry must be avoided, nevertheless, traditional learning communities must learn to cope with a student base which has, arguably, a shorter attention span than was true of preceding generations.

The third type of community is made up of the mass media, especially the audio-visual media, where television continues to have a significant role. This educational experience is essentially global and represents the link between ourselves and the world beyond our daily lived experience. It plays a vital role in our opening up to the world, in our becoming aware of belonging to a common humanity and in helping us get to know and recognise it in its multiplicity of expressions and works.

It was this which led Marshall McLuhan to substitute the expression 'global village' with that of 'global theatre' thus indicating that we are all, as it were, actors involved in each others' lives and not simply spectators.[5] These media act as genuine teachers (good or bad), as educational channels but also as filters of what can reach us. It is common to refer to journalists as the gatekeepers of the reality of the world which reaches us, acting also as interpreters of events and their meaning—a role formerly played by the teacher.

Of course besides their obvious educational role, the audio-visual media also play a role in entertaining us, amazing us and helping us relax from the demands of our daily work. For this reason we rely on them for much of our entertainment. Besides granting us access to the world of facts and events, the media open up for us imaginary worlds. The creation of such worlds in literature and various other forms under the heading 'fiction' brings about, as Paul Ricoeur notes, the opening up of our horizons allowing us to enlarge and multiply—through fantasy and imagination—our experience of reality and immerse ourselves in other lives and stories and histories.[6] In the past this would have taken place through the oral tradition of storytelling or literature or theatre. Today it is primarily delivered via cinema, television, interactive games or on-line virtual worlds. Here too the educational experience is changing. The community gathered round the television screen in family homes or social settings is increasingly being replaced by solitary viewing using non-traditional devices. The shift from watching television on a traditional set, to watching it on multiple devices is directly correlated with age. The proportion of 18-24 year olds who watch a television set daily is significantly lower than those aged over 35. In direct contrast, almost a quarter of 18-24 year olds use their computer to watch television daily, which is significantly higher than those aged over 25. We note here an important evolution in the patterns of television viewing.[7]

The Media and Education

In education and in any form of learned knowledge, example plays a fundamental role. Whether they are aware of it or not, parents act as a role model for their children, teachers for their pupils, older workers for younger workers and so on. This insight helps us to analyse the deepest sense of every educational relationship. The growth of values in us is always, at least to some extent, based on imitation or example. The child learns his values seeing them lived out in the lives of his parents or other adults whom he knows and admires. It is usually a real human person with whom we are in contact (rather than a written discourse) who makes values visible and, knowingly or unknowingly, encourages us to make these values our own. Pope Francis has repeatedly stressed the need for authenticity on the part of Christians in the transmission of the Christian message and cites St Joseph as the perfect example of the coherent teacher: 'St Joseph educated Christ primarily with the example of a "just man", who knows that salvation does not come from the observance of the law, but by the grace of God, of his love and faithfulness.'[8] The challenge inherent in this has long been recognised by educationalists:

> In this age of extreme individualism, we have almost left out of view the mission of home as the first form of society, and the important bearing it has upon the formation of character. Its interests are not appreciated; its duties and privileges are neglected; husbands and wives do not fully realize their moral relation to each other; parents are inclined to renounce their authority; and children, brought up in a state of domestic libertinism, neither respect nor obey their parents as they should. The idea of human character as a development from the nursery to the grave, is not realized. Home as a preparation for both the state and the church, and its bearing, as such, upon the prosperity of both, are renounced as traditionary, and too old and stale to suit this age of mechanical progression and 'young Americanism'.[9]

It is salutary to note that these words were written in 1859! Naturally in their growth to adulthood, young people will learn to evaluate ideas in the light of their own experiences and encounters and will thus either make them their own or reject them. Nonetheless, educators are not alone in serving as role models. The media also propose to us personalities, both real or fictional, to whom we compare ourselves, consciously or unconsciously. The impact of the media in proposing these models is explained well by the authors of *La Sfida Educativa*: media-generated personalities or styles of behaviour enjoy a myth of prestige and glamour based on the source they come from; such personalities have an impact on our daily conversations, they provide the common subject matter for our discussions and they form part of our shared knowledge; the realism of the modern media creates what some experts have called a para-social relationship between spectator and personality, a sort of non-reciprocal intimacy. Even though there is no real relationship the viewer creates links with real or imaginary figures on the screen as though they were friends.[10]

This process can happen very early because, from the earliest years, children encounter through television, real and imaginary figures who subtly teach styles of behaviour and models of interpersonal relationships. In this way the mass media act as powerful agents of formation which educators can no longer ignore. It is a unique role in that they do not create a direct interpersonal relationship between the viewer and onscreen figure but create a network of relationships in the public at large.

Part of the socialising role of the media is very explicit, for example, in children's programmes or in public service broadcasting—coverage of national events or religious services which consciously aim to allow individual spectators to feel part of the wider celebration. Thus the constant appeals for audience participation and feedback through text message or email. More traditional programming involves the indirect transmission of values and models of behaviour through the choice of which news to broadcast, how it is presented, which fictional series are made and how the characters are cast, the format of interviews or talk shows and the personalities chosen for appearance.

Thus we (inadvertently) entrust to the media many of our human needs: company, intellectual stimulation, the avoidance of boredom. Furthermore, the media strongly influence our perception of reality, our ideas and our conversations. No longer then can television, the computer or the smartphone, be seen as neutral pieces of equipment which link us to the outside world or as domestic gadgets capable of informing us, teaching us and entertaining us. Today the media is becoming more and more a 'neighbourhood' we inhabit which directly influences our daily life and relationships. There is, in other words, a new kind of pervasive and all-encompassing power of the media of which we need to be aware.

Antonio Spadaro SJ puts it thus:

> Technology is the organization of matter according to a conscious human design, and therefore, belongs to man's spiritual being. We are called upon to understand its very nature as it relates to spiritual life. Obviously, technology remains ambiguous because man's freedom can just as easily serve evil, but it is exactly this possibility that highlights how technology's very nature is intrinsically linked to a world of possibilities regarding the spirit.[11]

Recognition of such wide-ranging forces can lead us to think that we remain powerless in the face of media influence. However this would be a mistake. The truth is that the media require the coming together of two freedoms and two decisions—that of the broadcaster to decide the content and the message (even though in doing so they may seek to interpret the expectations of the viewer and listener); and that of the recipient who has the freedom to either link in and expose himself to the messages of the broadcaster or not. It is not surprising then that when a more powerful interest overtakes us—we worry, we fall in love, or we are overwhelmed by work—our media consumption is immediately altered. The attraction of going on-line, listening to music, watching TV and surfing the Internet is still limited by the competition of real life! This is the real limit on the power of the broadcaster and Benedict XVI is clear in his warning of the need to prioritise real relationships over virtual ones:

> Who is my 'neighbour' in this new world? Does the danger exist that we may be less present to those whom we encounter in our everyday life? Is there is a risk of being more distracted because our attention is fragmented and absorbed in a world other than the one in which we live? Do we have time to reflect critically on our choices and to foster human relationships which are truly deep and lasting? It is important always to remember that 'virtual contact' cannot and must not take the place of direct human contact with people at every level of our lives. [12]

So we arrive now at the core of the question: to what extent are the media genuine protagonists in the educational process? Do they have an educational responsibility? Indeed, do they have a role in education? The answer to this requires us to recognise that education can only take place in an inter-personal relationship, in the context of a human relationship which implies not only the transmission but also the acquisition of knowledge and values. This involves not only the intellect but also emotions and affections. The key to the educational relationship is *reciprocity*—a relationship in which the educator and the one being educated are both caught up in a rich dialogic process.

Pope Francis captured this truth very effectively in his speech to mark the 2014 Plenary of the Congregation for Catholic Education:

> The profound changes that have led to the ever wider diffusion of multicultural societies require those who work in the school or university sector to be involved in educational itineraries involving comparison and dialogue, with a courageous and innovative fidelity that enables Catholic identity to encounter the various 'souls' of multicultural society.[13]

In this sense the ideal of humanity, the ideal outcome of education is not a programme or a definition which the parent imposes on the child and the teacher on the pupil but is rather a common effort which involves the educator just as much as the one being educated. Romano Guardini, the German theologian, in a short piece entitled: *La credibilità dell'educatore* observes as follows:

> Education's greatest power consists in the fact that I [the educator] put myself forward and work so as to develop. This is the vital point. It is the fact that I have to struggle to improve myself which gives credibility to my teacherly role among those I am educating.[14]

If education is, therefore, possible only in the context of an interpersonal relationship, the media can be said not to be direct protagonists in the educational process. If we reflect further, however, we realise that nothing of that which we communicate is without educational value, whether that comes about as the direct result of the communicator's efforts or, as can happen, without the communicator's awareness.

Because of the role that the media now have in all our lives and especially in the lives of the young, it is certainly fair to say that the media *interfere* in the educational process in that they can support it, sustain it or make it harder and riskier. Often parents and teachers speak of their frustration and powerlessness in the face of this new competition they face for their child's attention and respect as the media are an opponent with a certain glamour and, apparently, an unbeatable competitive edge. But in this case the issue is not the glamour or fascination of the opposition—namely the media—but the *credibility* of the adults, parents and teachers. It is only this—with all the risk, hard work and sacrifice that it necessarily involves—which makes effective education possible. The media with their power and their allure, which certainly shouldn't be undervalued, cannot be used as an alibi, to explain away the disorientation and unease which affects adults as well as young people.

The Credibility of the Media as Educators

The media present one form of narrative through news and current affairs and others through fictional programmes. Does it matter how this happens? Are there criteria for judging a 'good' representation and a 'bad' representation, can educators distinguish between a respectful representation of reality and a representation which tends to amplify and legitimise distorted models and experiences of personal, family and social life?

The authors of *La Sfida Educativa* answer this question by stating that two criteria have to be employed: First, try to tell the truth and second be orientated towards the human person.[15]

With regard to the first criterion, there is an idea abroad which is supported by various philosophers and sociologists, that the truth is the result of an agreement sustained by the majority of what appears to be true. Some analysts, spotting the dangers inherent in this concept, have tried to find some mechanism to prevent this *consensual truth* simply resulting in the imposition of the views of those who shout the loudest. They have suggested that ideally all should have an equal chance to communicate their ideas so that in public discussion the best and most rational argument might win the day.

Experience, however, shows us that the truths which have the greatest impact on public opinion largely depend (obviously with some limits and exceptions) on the power of the media which transmit them, or certainly on those media outlets which act as opinion leaders, resulting in a system in which these media voices can promote and almost impose certain ideas, themes and interpretations of life.

Referring to the relationship between truth and information, the sociologist, Niklas Luhmann, describing with great realism (and a touch of cynicism) the work of journalists and those involved in the communications industries has observed that in scientific circles truth is the criterion on which ideas are judged while in the media world, the principle criterion in the search for and broadcast of news is not truth but novelty. So the most important distinction therefore, in the news world is not between truth and non-truth but between the 'new' and the 'already known' with the latter having almost no value.[16]

This blatant substitution of truth by novelty cannot be accepted by rational societies, not only from a theoretical point of view but also from a practical one if we want to avoid entering into a world of endless mirrors and ultimate self-contradiction. Even in the perfectly legitimate and appropriate diversity of ways of looking at an event or a problem, we cannot lose sight of the fact that things exist objectively in a certain way and that good quality news tries to sincerely understand events, seeking to bring out the greatest possible number of background details, context and witnesses to explain how things actually are while trying to avoid limitations and distortions.

The second criterion which gives value to media communication is an underlying approach to the dignity of the human person. We cannot be indifferent to the way in which man and his life are represented. We can speak of man—and of human relationships such as friendship, love, affection but also conflict, hatred and resentment—in a way that is open to the richness and the complexity of humanity or we can do it in a more stereotypical and demeaning way. This is equally true in the fiction and non-fiction worlds. It is striking for example that the media, and television in particular, communicate almost exclusively the *language of emotion* so that the most unlikely situations are presented and interpreted in terms of emotion: whether that be through interviews with protagonists at major events or on talk shows, whether it be the world of sport or politics, the culture of emotions is propagated constantly, which doesn't help reflection or evaluation which might lead to a better understanding.

The result of this can be a dulling of critical capacity on the part of the media consumer. This can be identified in the educational context. At risk is that capacity to evaluate different lifestyles, ideals and ideas and distinguish what is good and just and desirable from that which is exploitative, destructive and unjust. In this regard, *La Sfida Educativa* identifies three sociological tendencies which can only be judged negatively:

- *The ideal of the spectacular*. This model confuses happiness and fulfilment with fame and notoriety. This can be classified as an exhibitionist identity or a thirst for fame almost as though this were a fundamental need of man. The 'X factor phenomenon' is a case in point.[17] In fact there is a fundamental need of mankind—which these tendencies subvert—to be acknowledged by others as unique individual. There is no need to have recourse to philosophy, psychology or sociology to realise that the need not to be *anyone* but to be *someone* is fundamental in any person's life.

- *The fascination of the negative.* It is well known that the media favour negativity in the selection of both fiction and non-fiction material—the idea that in news terms "bad news is good news"—in the sense that it can interest and capture an audience more readily. For this reason, stories and situations are prioritised which constitute a breaking of the rules, a deviation, a departure from the normal course of things. And since the criterion for selection is the negativity of a story, what emerges is a schedule of stories and depicted relationships which are both problematic and troubled, in which the characters are incapable of responding to their own needs and problems, making common currency the emotions of hatred, frustration and resentment. This distortion can end in tragedy and violence on- and off-screen because it suggests the idea that every family relationship, every friendship, every experience of love is a trap or a prison, a place of non-communication and coercion, a black hole in which freedom and individual expression are threatened.
- *The de-legitimisation of the figure of the adult.* If the media propose as models a range of characters and lifestyles which go against the ideals proposed by parents and teachers, this produces as a perhaps unintended consequence the questioning of the role of parents as figures of authority. This is the least noted but perhaps the most serious effect of media interference in the educational process. The pupil needs to believe in and respect the figure of the teacher just as the child needs to believe in and respect the role of the parents. This respect for adults is essential in the developing of a balanced personality and in establishing relations of trust with other people. The risk in over-exposure of young people to the media (more so if it starts early, lasts a long time,

> and is solitary with the child closed in a bedroom with a remote control, free from interruption from other members of the family) is that such exposure constitutes a distorted but powerful window for the child into the negative and sometimes dangerous world of adults. Watching news, sitcoms, drama series and talk shows (even those which don't appear to have anything worrying or dangerous about them), young people pick up in a rather crude and unsubtle way the idea that adults are corrupt, violent liars; that politicians are only out to feather their own nest; that husbands and wives constantly betray each other and that adults rob, kill and carry out acts of violence on a daily basis. The most serious aspect of this problem—this unfiltered viewing of a distorted version of adult life—is that it usually happens when the child is too young have in place the necessary internal filters to be able to distinguish between fiction and real life.

A consequence of this could be that young people develop a tendency for disillusionment and lack of trust, leading to their calling into question the values and lifestyles which their parents and teachers propose to them. Such models and the values are, according to the incessant voice of the media, only a fiction and not really practical. The tragedy is that this casts a cloud of suspicion over all of adult life and the family comes to be seen as a facade behind which is hidden a reality of insincerity, dysfunction and violence.

New Media

If it is true that the traditional media still play a major role in information and entertainment and TV remains a dominant medium, it cannot be denied that the media panorama is changing dramatically, largely through the emergence of the new media and the uses which can be made of it, especially by our young people.

It is difficult to define new media because it is an entire communications world constantly in movement and ever-evolving. Perhaps it is best to define it as those media which are based on the twin base of computer technology and tele-communication. Facebook, Twitter, Flicker and Instagram lead the way but variants are always emerging. The New Media are pervasive: they penetrate every space of our personal life, at home and in the street and they accentuate that view of the media which sees it as not only a technological area but also a social and cultural area. The *modus operandi* of the new media can be described as follows:

- the New Media favour interaction and facilitates the active intervention of users, from the basic option of choosing a TV channel to more sophisticated interaction via internet and hand-held devices. The user hence becomes a participant, breaking the rigid division of roles based on the model of the few (broadcasters) servicing the many (a multiplicity of consumers);
- the New Media allow the sharing of digital content leading to the instant and often free access to information which can be downloaded, manipulated and redistributed without cost. This is now the norm;
- the New Media favour sharp and targeted opinion over thoughtful and discursive discourse. Twitter, for example, with its 140 character limit, is particularly guilty of fostering sharp and destructive exchanges;
- the New Media with their focus on self expression blur the private/public sphere and can endanger users who are imprudent, often unintenionally, in their postings;
- the individuals in charge of websites, blogs, social networking or online generated resources, such as *Wikipedia*, are enormous influences in shaping the social and cultural agenda.

In his message for Communications Day 2014 Pope Francis sums up these dangers well:

> The speed with which information is communicated exceeds our capacity for reflection and judgement, and this does not make for more balanced and

> proper forms of self-expression. The variety of opinions being aired can be seen as helpful, but it also enables people to barricade themselves behind sources of information which only confirm their own wishes and ideas, or political and economic interests. The world of communications can help us either to expand our knowledge or to lose our bearings. The desire for digital connectivity can have the effect of isolating us from our neighbours, from those closest to us. We should not overlook the fact that those who for whatever reason lack access to social media run the risk of being left behind.[18]

Nonetheless, it is important not to be unduly negative regarding the new ways of communicating. Perhaps the most positive educational implication of all of this, for the Catholic educator, is the capacity of the new digital media to create new communities by responding to the human need for relationship and participation. This dimension can be summed up in the term 'friendship': the key word of the social networks and the word users of these networks use to describe the relationship formed between them. (A 'Facebook Friend' may be someone the user has never met, whose voice would never be recognised, whose background and values are unknown.) From an educational point of view, learning is not confined to the relationship between parent and child, teacher and pupil, experienced worker and apprentice. It can also be carried out among equals in the context of a 'friend relationship'. Friendship is educational and online friendship can have this role too. Once again Francis is accurate in his summation of the situation:

> It is not enough to be passers-by on the digital highways, simply 'connected'; connections need to grow into true encounters. We cannot live apart, closed in on ourselves. We need to love and to be loved. We need tenderness. Media strategies do not ensure beauty, goodness and truth in communication. The world of media also has to be concerned with humanity, it too is called to show tenderness.

> The digital world can be an environment rich in humanity; a network not of wires but of people.[19]

The important thing, however, is not the capacity to build relationships online but the quality of the relationship which is created between people and the quality of the conversations which they share. It is important not to minimise or undervalue the importance of just 'being together' which all the studies show to be the most important and satisfying thing for young people and adolescents in their use of social networks. It is important however that this 'being together'—online as much as in real life—should not simply be the habitation of a vacuum, the forum for a repetition of banalities, the source of alienation or degradation or a stimulus to transgression as a result of boredom.

The problem is not the fact that online we can find anything we want and meet anyone we want. The real issue is to know what to look for: how to avoid our search being meaningless and instead give it some sort of direction. This 'direction' cannot come from the web as such, and cannot be found there. It comes rather from real values imbued as a result of real relationships with real people who live in real places and establish true educative and affectionate bonds. Herein lies a challenge for the Catholic educator.

Having this formation helps young people to be alert to the risks of casual encounters online. In today's society, online relationships with people we do not know are growing fast and as a result we are seeing a radical shift in our standards of credibility and trust. The dangers of online encounters can be categorised as follows: in the first place, there are encounters with the *bad teachers* who spread extreme and violent political ideas, disseminate hatred, preach intolerance, distribute pornography and encourage online corruption and all forms of scams. There are also encounters with the *false friends* who come disguised and who can be in some situations the most dangerous of presences online: sites where content that was not requested pops up, sites offering gifts or free services which are not really free and the invasive and omnipresent publicity designed for nefarious results like identity theft, paedophile grooming or fraud.

There are also other risks linked to the possibility of establishing new media educational relationships that are essentially distorted and indeed poisoned. We see this in the narcissism which manifested in the exhibitionist and show-off tendency which can sometimes be found on personal blogs or on certain uses of Facebook. In addition, the acceptance of 'false identity'—or the use of nicknames which allow the possibility of sending photos or images which hide one's true identity—is not without its problems. If on one hand this can create a link which is free of risk and involvement, on the other hand it exposes people to the risk of being duped and of perverse developments. Finally, increasing numbers of young people are seeking refuge online as an escape from the pressures and demands of daily life. There are real pathologies associated with substituting online life for real life as in the well-documented case of thousands of young Japanese shutting themselves up in their own homes, drastically reducing their exposure to the external world and communicating exclusively through new media. Psychologists are beginning to report similar behaviour patterns in Europe and other parts of Asia. Indeed, researchers in Norway have published a new psychological scale to measure Facebook addiction, the first of its kind worldwide.[20]

Despite these risks there are important new opportunities which show the positive side of the new media. First, online socialisation is not usually vertical (from one generation to another) but is rather horizontal among people of the same generation. This allows younger people to have a direct involvement and awareness in establishing their own form of communication. This doesn't happen automatically or spontaneously, rather an educational element is required, offering testimonials and giving examples of good practice so as to make the best possible use of the opportunities opened by digital media.

Neither can we discount the role of new technologies in assisting the personal growth and self esteem among young people. The recognition and valuing of young people's skills by the adults in the household, and also by groups and associations who recognise young people's key roles and skills in new media, is a positive development.

Finally, new media can faciliate new and more attractive forms of participation in civic and democratic life. They can give new access to news and current affairs and can allow people to have their voice heard either as individuals or as groups and thus contribute positively to the great debates of the age, be they ethical, political or social.

Media Responsibility

What we read, listen to and see via the media is not solely dependent on market forces, rather content is also developed and produced by a professional and cultural elite made up of journalists, politicians, campaigners, authors, producers and directors. It is they, through the choices they make, who shape the content for media consumption.

The authors of *La Sfida Educativa* suggest that it is important to be guided by a *principle of precaution.* This principle is already well grounded in European legislation in areas such as environmental policy, healthcare and consumers' rights.[21] The European Union puts it thus:

> The principle of precaution can be invoked when an urgent intervention is required as a result of possible danger to human health, animal or vegetable well-being, or for the protection of the environment in cases where scientific data do not allow a full evaluation of the risk factors. This principle is to be applied especially in situations of danger to the health of the human person. This would allow, for example, a ban to be placed on the distribution of

> products which may be dangerous to human health or the withdrawal of such products from the market."

We can also ask why this same principle cannot be applied to media products which may prove to be dangerous to psychological well-being or human relationships. Why not apply this principle to the media world, to the world of human ecology bearing in mind the developing scientific research which is beginning to demonstrate linkage between exposure to violence in the media and the phenomenon of bullying as a result of copying behavioural types seen in the media?

This principle of precaution should not solely be applied by professionals in the communication industry but also by consumers. It should be applied by public authorities and educationalists, by civil society, by the Church, by families and by users of the media, young and old alike.

However, this principle of precaution is a negative; it emphasises the need for vigilance with regard to dangers linked to media exposure. As such it is insufficient. It needs to be completed and augmented by a more active and positive programme of choices on the part of all involved—producers and consumers alike. Ideally one would want a deliberate desire for the good which recognises in the risk of communication an opportunity to be treasured.

While this responsibility is primarily one for the political decision-makers, it is shared by those who work in the communications industries. The quality of communication cannot depend exclusively on external controls but should rather be based on a freely shared set of values and standards which communications workers—proprietors, professional employees and investors—should see as an honourable pact between themselves and the public.[22]

There is also a role for individual responsibility on the part of those working in the media. The quality and content of the media we consume remain largely the result of the positive (or negative) choices of those who work in that industry. For this reason there is a great responsibility to promote the education and formation of those who work in this industry. On the one hand this involves universities and journalism schools but, on the other, it is essential that from within society itself—starting with the Church—there should be a constant search and encouragement of young people with a particular vocation to this area.

In this way the world of education becomes an active participant in the shaping of news agendas. If the key issue remains that of the credibility of the teacher, of his ability to transmit knowledge, to make his own the expectations and difficulties of the pupils, to be attentive and involved in a genuine educational relationship, one instrument (among others) which educational establishments should make available to their students is the development of a competency in communications as an integral part of their cultural development. This may involve the insertion of media education into the curriculum - understood not only as familiarisation with the language of the media - but also as the development of a critical autonomy and the capacity to use the media to form opinions on events, problems and social processes which allow individuals to judge and decide for themselves.

Concluding Remarks

Families remain the primary context for the educational relationship. Thus there is a need to equip families so that they too can extend their educational role to include assistance in positive and critical use of the media which should be seen as supports, not enemies, of the correct rearing of children. This implies the use of a strategy of defence of the family from external dangers—a vigilance with a special awareness of the dangers inherent in exposing the youngest children to inappropriate and dangerous content—but it also requires an engagement within the family, accompanying young people and sharing to some extent their viewing and listening habits. Families have to move from one strategy to the other based on the maturing of the young people, their growing capacity for interaction with the media and their ability to understand better and evaluate better the messages that come from television and other media sources.

To provide effective tools for this task, parishes, associations, movements and other Church groups can, and should, consider running formation courses and events which allow an opportunity for reflection for parents on how they use the media and how the media can be usefully engaged within the family unit.

The level of activity of locally-based associations and groups are widely perceived to be indicators of the health of society. An array of associations, movements, clubs and meeting places is essential to allow people to establish bonds of solidarity and reciprocity, and they also help people develop a reflective capacity and a critical judgement about events and experiences including experience of media consumption.

Western society is well supplied with such groupings, present within the Church—parishes, dioceses, associations, movements—and also within wider society (cultural associations, political parties, volunteer groups, sporting associations etc.) These can act as a filter promoting a selective, critical and conscious use of the media. They can also act as promoters of new means of communication based closer to the societies they serve, promoting wider access, through involvement and participation in both the more traditional media but also taking advantage of the many opportunities offered by the new media.

Educational establishments in particular can and should include in their life a web presence and social media life which is both creative and fully aware of the importance of communicating their own identity and values. In this way, *real* communities can play a vital role in humanising society. We conclude this chapter with the hope-filled words of Pope Francis:

> Only those who go out of themselves in their communication can become a true point of reference for others. Personal engagement is the basis of the trustworthiness of a communicator. Christian witness, thanks to the Internet, can thereby reach the peripheries of human existence.[23]

Notes

1 *La Sfida Educativa* (Rome: Editori Laterza, 2009), Chapter 8.

2 Pope Francis, *Message for World Communications Day* (2014)

3 A. Zukowski, *The Digital Continent and Catholic Education*. The complete text is available at: http://www.ncea.org/UserFiles/File/Communications/SepOct09Technology.pdf.

4 Pope Benedict XVI, *Discourse at the Inauguration of the Convention of the Diocese of Rome* (11 June 2007); Pope Francis, *Discourse to Pontifical Council for Justice and Peace* (3 October 2013).

5 This theme is developed considerably in M. McLuhan and B. Powers, *The Global Village: Transformations in World Life and Media in the 21st Century* (New York/Oxford: Oxford University Press, 1989).

6 P. Ricoeur, *Time and Narrative Volume 1* (Chicago: University Of Chicago Press, 1990).

7 YouGov Report. *Changing Media Summit* (London 2013). The complete text is available at:http://cdn.yougov.com/cumulus_uploads/document/jrlh273vq2/YG-G-Changing-Media-Summit-Report-PARTI.pdf.

8 Pope Francis, *General Audience* (19 March 2014).

9 S. Philips, *The Christian Home*, Project Gutenberg eBook http://www.gutenberg.org/files/14237/14237-h/14237-h.htm.

10 *La Sfida Educativa* (2009) chapter 8.

11 A. Spadaro SJ, *Cybergrace: Spirituality in the Age of Internet*. Digital Edition http://www.amazon.com/dp/B00CAT9E8I/.

12 Pope Benedict XVI, *Message for World Communications Day* (2011).

13 Pope Francis, *Address to Plenary Assembly Congregation for Catholic Education* (13 Feb 2014). See Appendix 2 of this volume for the complete text.

14 R. Guardini, *La Credibilità dell'educatore* (*The Credibility of the Educator*). The full text of this short article is available at: at: http://www.donboscoland.it/articoli/articolo.php?id=123662.

15 *La Sfida Educativa* (2009) Chapter 8.

16 Cf N. Luhmann, *The Reality of the Mass Media: Cultural Memory in the Present* (Translated by Kathleen Cross) (Oxford: Blackwell, 2000).

17 The *X Factor* is a British TV programme which works as a singing talent competition. Members of the public face weeks of auditions

before the winner is finally decided by a public vote. Since it began in 2004, the show has been the subject of increasing criticism and controversy, mostly in reference to its negative effects on the quality and reputation of the British music industry.

18 Pope Francis, *Message for World Communications Day* (2014).

19 *Ibid.*

20 The lead researcher, Dr Cecilie Andraessen of the University of Bergen (UiB), said: 'We have also found that people who are anxious and socially insecure use Facebook more than those with lower scores on those traits, probably because those who are anxious find it easier to communicate via social media than face-to-face.' The Norwegian team also finds that people who are more organized and ambitious tend not to become addicted to Facebook, and are more likely to use social media as an integral part of work and networking activity.http://www.medicalnewstoday.com/articles/245251.php.

21 See http://europa.eu/legislation_summaries/consumers/consumer_safety/l32042_en.htm.

22 This relationship between owners, producers and consumers of the media was the focus of a long-running and revelatory inquiry in the UK in 2012 under the supervision of Lord Justice Leveson. An Executive Summary of the *Leveson Report* is available at: http://www.official-documents.gov.uk/document/hc1213/hc07/0779/0779.asp.

23 Pope Francis, *Message for World Communications Day* (2014).

4

THE ITALIAN CONTEXT

Few Catholic initiatives in recent years have been quite so well developed in their theory and extensive in their outreach as the *Progetto* of the Catholic Bishops' Conference of Italy, born in the mid 1990s when John Paul II memorably called them to a new approach in their pastoral work—a call for no less than a 'moral and cultural rebirth of society'.

The *Progetto* is essentially a way of allowing the Church to engage with modern society from within. No longer is the ecclesial community seen as a city on a hill, illuminating the secular valley below. Rather society is envisaged as a *piazza* around which a variety of world views compete for attention. Indeed the *Progetto*'s logo is of a stylised piazza based on the famous *Piazza del Palio* in Siena with its recognisable buildings representing the Church, the law courts and civic governance. The Church's role, as envisaged by the *Progetto,* is to *propose,* not *impose,* its wisdom, vision and anthropology to all who throng the piazza of everyday life, confident in the life-changing beauty of its Gospel-based content.

It is unarguable that Christianity no longer has the profound influence on European society and its institutions that it once had and it is in full recognition of this state of affairs that the *Progetto* operates. The disengagement between Church and state is best tackled, we argue, at a local level: the *Progetto* seeks to encourage local initiatives to grow organically according to the circumstances and needs of each city/institution/region. This insight, of course, has a universal relevance. For example when a threat is made to close a school or parish or care home, those directly affected at a local level quickly and effectively respond, organising committees, seeking alliances, proposing their message to a sympathetic public. In doing so they 'create culture'. Disengagement quickly disappears when local grass roots initiatives with decent resources and a compelling message are established. Accordingly, since the *Progetto* is very clearly not a one-size-fits-all pastoral plan, its insights and methodology in *creating culture* can be of interest to Catholic educators far beyond the Italian context. This chapter describes the various levels at which the *Progetto* operates and argues that it is a creative means of reshaping Catholic education's encounter with the world of culture.

The Workings of the Progetto Culturale

It is perhaps opportune at this point to define what the cultural project *is* and, more importantly, *is not*. Its understanding of culture is not that of high artistic achievement. It is neither an expensive chaplaincy for opera, ballet or classic drama nor a cunning 'master plan' to reclaim the worlds of music, drama, literature and art for the Church. It does not represent an attempt by the bishops to control institutes of culture or higher learning. Rather the 'cultural' function of the *Progetto* is understood in its widest sense. Culture is, in the words of John Paul II, 'that privileged terrain where the faith meets mankind'.[1] It is the everyday experience of the Christian, the influences, the ideas, the context in which he or she operates. It is to be seen not as an enemy of faith but rather as the terrain which will produce better fruits when its land is irrigated by the Christian message.

This understanding of culture has serious implications, not only for wider society, but for the Church itself. John Paul II stated this powerfully in his memorable phrase that 'a faith which does not become culture is a faith which has not been fully welcomed, not properly thought out and not faithfully lived out.'[2] The novelty, so to speak, of the *Progetto* is that it explicitly makes the effort at inculturation within the context of Western societies whose DNA has become increasingly, and essentially, secular. In this sense evangelisation and inculturation are seen as different yet wholly related concepts. The Gospel is the key message of both in the promotion of a truly human culture.

Since its foundation in Italy in the mid 1990s, the *Progetto* has developed into a vast network of persons, publications, events, plans and initiatives. It has directly or indirectly given birth to a respected TV channel (TV2000) and a new form of digital engagement (www.testimonidigitali.it). Its extraordinary publishing initiative (*La Sfida Educativa*), the key text on education, was launched by the Education Minister of the Italian state, published by a secular publisher and ran to its 10th edition within a year of publication. The *Progetto* is responsible for organising sacred theatre festivals (*I teatri del sacro*), and national conferences, bringing together Catholic and secular voices to reflect on important national anniversaries as well as major international events on the great unspoken issues of the day. A notable contribution to the *Progetto* was the conference in 2009 entitled *God Today: Presence or Absence Changes Everything* (*Dio Oggi con Lui O Senza Di Lui Cambia Tutto*) which brought together distinguished thinkers from the Catholic and atheist worlds to discuss the fundamental question of God's existence.[3]

The *Progetto* has a relatively simple structure: a *National Committee* headquartered in Rome with responsibility for organising major conferences and national initiatives, and a *Service* operating across the country which links local cultural centres, universities and dioceses. It offers support for conferences, publications, events, think tanks, reflection groups and local publishing initiatives.

This structure represents a bold departure for the Italian Church from previous models of pastoral care which could be summed up, perhaps unfairly, as follows: precise, theological education for the élite and popular devotions for the masses. The *Progetto* model, on the other hand, is very much aligned to the spirituality of the lay apostolate which emerged from the Second Vatican Council. In this way of thinking, the good fruits of theological and anthropological research grow organically from the grass roots, thus helping inform and 'create' culture.[4]

Progetto Culturale: *A New Way of Encounter*

Within the Christian community the construction of culture should be first and foremost based on popular culture. As part of the life of the Church, this should involve everyone and form part of pastoral activity resulting also at a local level in the promotion of events, encounters and pastoral action. The *Progetto* is a great resource in bringing closer together the life of the Church and the day-to-day existence and questions of ordinary people: this creates a space for dialogue without any inferiority complexes and in harmony with the cultural norms of the age. This is no easy task but it is a fascinating adventure which is worth the effort to give a new energy to the culture of our time and to restore the Christian faith's full right of citizenship to the world of culture.

In their Pastoral Guidelines (*Orientamenti*) for 2010-2020, the Italian Bishops' Conference set out their vision of the *Progetto.* Importantly, they used a term, 'self-referential', which Pope Francis would frequently employ in his addresses:

> Only a community which is welcoming and open to dialogue can succeed in establishing bonds of friendship and offering answers to the thirst for God which is present in the heart of every human being. Today it is necessary to find new languages, not self-referential, and enriched with the contributions of the world of communication, art and culture. For this reason, education must lead to a more motivated faith, capable of dialogue even with those who engage with the Church only occasionally, with believers in other religions and with non-believers.[5]

From the beginning the *Progetto* created opportunities for an encounter between those who, in various ways, work in the cultural sector and those who come to it as believers. It recognised the need to overcome the separation between so-called high culture and popular culture and thus in all its efforts tried to bridge this false and harmful gap. One means of doing this was the Forum of the cultural project. This series of eleven gatherings between October 1997 and December 2012 focussed on relevant themes for a teaching Church immersed in a society in constant renewal. It is enough to look at the eleven topics to get a flavour of the current thought among Catholic intellectuals. Among the issues discussed, and later produced as an attractive series of books, are the following titles: Catholicism and the Future of the Country; The Council 40 years on: Christian Teaching Today; Religious Freedom and Cultural Change; Europe: Challenge for Catholics; Rethinking the Parish; The 150 years since the Unity of Italy; The Future of Mankind: Christian Faith and Anthropology; Demographic Change and Work and From Generation to Generation: The Difficult Construction of the Future.

Right from the outset it was acknowledged by the advocates of the *Progetto* that reflection and discussion had to be accompanied by action.[6] The aim was not to ask dioceses to create a new curial department but rather to co-ordinate better the various initiatives which were already taking place in the fields of evangelisation and culture. For this reason, a network of Catholic cultural centres was established: in 2013 this involved 415 such centres. The *Progetto* has created a new linkage between them and assists individual centres in the planning, programming and publicising of their initiatives. Such cultural centres cover a wide variety of institutions—parish associations, institutes run by religious orders, study centres, libraries and conferences organised by Catholic associations. One unexpected outcome has been the rebirth of the phenomenon of parish community halls based on the older custom of the parish cinema but now offering a much more extensive cultural programme.

Understandably, the co-ordination of such a mission has not been without its challenges. Results have not been universally positive since the creation of any new network requires each group or association to work together. Despite the initial problems, today almost every Italian diocese has a cultural project presence. Some of the initiatives have been dramatic and made national news. Others (perhaps the more important result) work away quietly to affect positively the culture of the local area. It certainly can be argued that the ethos of the *Progetto* has changed the way Italian Catholics think—the realisation has dawned that any initiative has to take into account the cultural context in which it is to operate and therefore the study of that local culture is now seen as a necessary preliminary step. In a broader context, the message of *proposing* rather than *imposing* the Christian message is better understood and more widely accepted.

In the years since it was born, the *Progetto* has collaborated with individuals and institutions from different faith and cultural backgrounds. This has required a delicate balancing act which requires both openness to dialogue with a variety of cultural strands and at the same time a solid link to Catholic identity. This has been done successfully at both national and diocesan levels. The architects of the project like to speak of their work in terms of a great 'shipyard' or building site which brings together men and women of different faiths and of social backgrounds to work for the common good.

This inspiration draws heavily from the definition of culture proposed in the great Magna Carta document of Vatican II, *Gaudium et Spes,* which encouraged the Church to consider the so-called 'anthropological' question, and a closer engagement with those issues which impact on the daily lives of persons, families and society. This 'anthropological' question is closely linked to the 'God' question with its implications for the human person and the issues of truth, personal behaviour and societal choices.

World of Communications

Over the years, the *Progetto* put special emphasis on the need for good communication and an intelligent and positive presence of Catholics in the media. This has led to the involvement of the *Progetto* and its personnel in areas such as *Avvenire* (the newspaper of the Italian Bishops' Conference), *TV2000* (the Italian Catholic TV channel) and *Sir* (the religious news agency). There has also been widespread collaboration with the network of local Catholic titles and initiatives such as theatre festivals, involvement in the great Turin and Bologna book fairs, the development of its website and the publication of over 200 new books.

The effort to engage with wider society work coincides with the vision of Pope Francis of a Church which goes out from itself. His address to lay movements in 2013 picked up the theme of openness:

> At this moment of crisis we can't worry only about ourselves, close ourselves in our own loneliness and discouragement and feel impotent when faced with the problems around us. Please do not close in on yourselves! This is a danger. We close ourselves inside the parish in groups of friends, a religious movement, with people who think the same way as we do… but do you know what happens? When the Church closes in on itself it gets sick, it gets ill. Think about a room sealed for a year; when you go in there is a smell of dampness. It doesn't feel good. A Church closed in on itself is the same thing; it is a stale Church; it is a sick Church. The Church must go out from itself.[7]

These words provide a fitting context to, and commentary on, the *Progetto*'s contribution to educational thought.

The **Progetto Culturale** *and Education*

In 2009, the Italian bishops highlighted education as the key area for engagement of the Church in general and the

Progetto in particular over the subsequent decade. This choice has meant that the lessons and fruits of the cultural project, with its considerable resources and huge network of participants, has become a powerful exemplar and laboratory for all who wish to explore the place of Catholic education in secular society.

The introduction to the cultural project's key text on education, *La Sfida Educativa,* cites the insights of sociologist Emile Durkheim:

> What is needed is education and professionals capable of teaching. But it is difficult to find one or the other if there is no patrimony of values and wisdom, no tradition considered worth transmitting.[8]

Cardinal Camillo Ruini (along with John Paul II, the founder, father figure and inspiration of the *Progetto*) has noted that education is a primordial and global human process, in which the fundamental structures of human existence come into play with implications for relationships and especially the need for love. Benedict XVI summed up this line of thinking very precisely in the now famous discourse on education known as the *Letter to the Diocese of Rome* where he noted that the actual root of the crisis in education is a crisis of faith in life itself. [9] For Pope Benedict, the *educational emergency* is inevitable in a society in which relativism is dominant because such a worldview removes from society's understanding the light of truth. It condemns every person to cast doubt on the worth and good of his or her own life and hence casts doubt too on the value of working with others to create something lasting and worthwhile.[10]

In turn, Francis has repeatedly called, as we have seen, for a less self-referential Church that is credible in its testimony. His call for authenticity and credibility of witness is a natural development of and response to Benedict's diagnosis of a so-called educational emergency:

> The results of our pastoral work do not depend on a wealth of resources, but on the creativity of love. To

> be sure, perseverance, effort, hard work, planning and organization all have their place, but first and foremost we need to realize that the Church's power does not reside in herself; it is hidden in the deep waters of God, into which she is called to cast her nets.[11]

The teaching of Francis sheds a new light on the crucial relationship between teacher and pupil which is at the heart of the 'educational emergency'. During his tenure as Archbishop of Buenos Aires, he maintained the custom of celebrating a Mass for Education in Holy Week, and would use the occasion to comment on the issues facing educators. During these addresses, he repeatedly focussed on the dialogue between teacher and student. In typically direct style he challenged educators to leave behind their closed texts to focus more on the student than on the curriculum:

> Do we have a heart which is open enough to let ourselves be surprised every day by the creativity of children, by their dreams? Do I let myself be surprised by the child's experiences? Do I let myself be surprised by the transparency of the child? Do I allow myself to wonder at the thousand and one antics of the little ones who are in our classrooms? Do I have a heart that is open or closed? Am I locked in a kind of museum of acquired knowledge and teaching methods where everything is perfect and where I see my role as being to impose but not receive anything? As an educator, do I have a receptive and humble heart to see the freshness of a child? If I don't, something very serious can happen: I will get stale. If the parent or educator has a rancid closed heart, the boy of the Gospel is left with his five loaves and the two fish without knowing to whom to give them to, he is frustrated in his disappointment, his desire for solidarity is thwarted.[12]

This almost lyrical passage echoes the quote from Italian author Natalia Ginzburg which is placed right at the beginning of the first chapter of *La Sfida Educativa*:

> This is perhaps the only real chance we have to help young people succeed, to help them in their choice of vocation—to do this we need to have a vocation ourselves, we need to know it, to love it and serve it with passion: because love for life generates love for life.[13]

Over the years the *Progetto* has been second to none in creative engagement with society, providing numerous opportunities for the evangelical witness so central to Pope Francis's world view to be encountered in an attractive, not an aggressive way. The programme for 2013-2014 is typical of what can be achieved in any society capable of adapting this model of educational and evangelical engagement to its own norms and customs. It begins with the following words of Pope Francis:

> The great spiritual questions of today are more alive than ever but we need people who can interpret them and understand them with intelligence, humility and openness—'To search and find God in all things' as St Ignatius wrote. God is at work in the life of every man and culture. The spirit blows where he will. Try to discover what God has done and how to carry out his work.
>
> It is also necessary to pay particular attention to truth, goodness and the duty of God, which should always be taken together, and our precious allies in the task of defending human dignity in the creation of peaceful co-existence and in safeguarding creation. The result of this is a serene, sincere and clear ability to judge events in the light of Christ. All of this requires that hearts and minds remain open, avoiding at all costs the spiritual disease of being self-referential.[14]

Concluding Remarks

The wisdom of the *Progetto* has it that within the Christian community the construction of culture should involve everyone and form part of pastoral activity resulting even at a local level in the promotion of events, encounters and pastoral action. The *Progetto* is a great resource in bringing closer together the life of the Church and the day-to-day existence and questions of ordinary people creating a space for dialogue without any inferiority complexes and in harmony with the cultural norms of the age. This is not an easy task but it is 'a fascinating adventure that is worth our effort, to give a new thrust to the culture of our time and to restore the Christian faith to full citizenship in it.'[15]

The following quote sums up the educational insight of the *Progetto*:

> The cultural project should stimulate in every baptised person in every community a deepening of faith and a strong sense that faith has a fully legitimate role in our society and can contribute to society's growth. [16]

This vision, though first planted in the soil of Dante and Petrarch, can surely bear fruit in the cultures of all societies.

Notes

1 Pope John Paul II, *To the Italian Church on the Occasion of its Third Ecclesial Conference in Palermo* (23 November 1995). (Italian only.)

2 Pope John Paul II, *To Participants in the National Congress of the Ecclesial Movements for Cultural Commitment* (16 January 1982). (Italian and Portuguese only.)

3 A short report on the conference is available at http://www.chiesacattolica.it/chiesa_cattolica_italiana/news_e_mediacenter/00009131_Dio_Oggi._Con_Lui_o_senza_di_Lui_cambia_tutto.html.

4 Pope Francis, *Address to the Community of Writers of La Civiltà Cattolica* (14 June 2013).

5 Catholic Bishops' Conference of Italy, *Educare alla Vita Buona del Vangelo* 41. The full text of this important document is available (in Italian) at: http://www.chiesacattolica.it/documenti/2010/10/00015206_educare_alla_vita_buona_del_vangelo_orien.html.

6 The *Progetto Culturale* is managed locally by a diocesan representative.

7 Pope Francis, *Meeting with Lay Movements for Year of Faith* (18 May 2013).

8 *La Sfida Educativa* (2009), p. xiv.

9 Pope Benedict XVI, *Letter to the Faithful of the Diocese and City of Rome on the Urgent Task of Educating Young People* (21 January 2008).

10 Pope Benedict XVI, *To the Participants in the Ecclesial Diocesan Convention of Rome* (6 June 2005).

11 Pope Francis, *Message to Bishops of Brazil* (27 July 2013).

12 Jorge Bergoglio/Pope Francis, Homily at Mass for Education (18 April 2007). The full text (in Spanish) is available at: http://www.quenoserepita.com.ar/homilia_de_monsenor_bergoglio_en_la_misa_por_la_educacion.

13 *La Sfida Educativa* (2009), Chapter 1.

14 Pope Francis, *Discourse to staff of La Civiltà Cattolica* (14 June 2013).

15 Pope Benedict XVI, *Discourse to the Participants in the Fourth National Ecclesial Convention of Verona* (19 October 2006).

16 Catholic Bishops' Conference of Italy, *Educare alla Vita Buona del Vangelo* 41.

5

LOOKING AHEAD: THE CATHOLIC SCHOOL AS A CULTURAL PROJECT

THE *PROGETTO* IS the first significant educational initiative of the Italian Church since the Second Vatican Council. This might seem surprising given the considerable body of Magisterial documents on education and catechesis published since that major event in the history of Christianity. At the heart of the Italian Bishops' educational concerns is a declared lack of trust in the understanding and operation of 'authority', understood as a source of life and growth.[1] This stated concern is manifested in the difficulties faced by the Italian Church in its desire to transform contemporary culture in the light of the Christian Gospel. In this vision, there emerges an understanding of education which is, rightly, broader than schooling but has a clear impact on Catholic school systems.

The *Progetto* is a direct and far-reaching response to an Italian sociological and cultural reality. Given the unconditional Italian flavour of the *Progetto,* we need to consider if its key ideas and approach are transferable—and how—to other educational, cultural and religious contexts. Is it reasonable to suggest that the ways of working adopted by the Catholic Church in Italy may be, with the necessary cultural and linguistic modifications, a template for other local Churches?

The question becomes more acute in the case of the Anglo-Saxon world where public attitudes to Catholicism since the Reformation have been marked by implicit and explicit suspicion of Catholic ways. Of course, this suspicion is not all one way as the history of post-Reformation Europe reveals. The legacy of anti-Catholicism in the Anglosphere would suggest that any reconfiguration of the *Progetto* would require careful planning and a nuanced religious and cultural sensitivity. Nonetheless, we maintain that the key ideas emergent from the *Progetto* can be reshaped to influence positively the culture of the Catholic school in the Anglophone West as elsewhere. In particular, the stated purpose of education as outlined in the *Progetto* offers a mechanism for taking forward cultural dialogue across a variety of international and religious contexts.

The transferability of the *Progetto* comes from its focus on the importance of education as a wide-ranging and rich engagement with culture. The distinctiveness of Catholic education lies in its unique approach to pedagogy and the place of cultural knowledge in the life of its network of educational institutions. In this chapter we will look first at the conceptual framework of Catholic education which emerges from reflection on the *Progetto*. Following this we will briefly explore some new initiatives in the Catholic world before arguing that Catholic education, broadly understood, is the new *Paideia* for the contemporary Church. Finally, we will give selected examples of how this vision can be put into practice.

The **Progetto Culturale***: A Model for Catholic Education*

The *Progetto*'s vision of education is not a direct product of Catholic theological thinking. Some may find this fact surprising given that it is a key factor in the Church in Italy's desire to promote a renewal of Christianity. The *Progetto*'s educational wing, so to speak, is principally a philosophically-conditioned response to the anthropological questions arising from the nature of authority as expressed in education, the family and in society (see above). According to the literature of the *Progetto*, the role of the teacher as figure of 'authority' has to be reclaimed from a misunderstanding of authority as a form of repression of individual freedom of the young.[2] The Latin root of authority—*augere* (to increase, to give birth to) and its derivative *auctoritas*—allows us to propose the proper use of authority as the means of growth: a teacher with authority is one who assists young people to grow into mature and wise human beings.[3]

According to Cardinal Ruini, the *sfida*, or the educational challenge, is best understood as an unwillingness to conceptualise education as cross-generational cultural transmission, as was understood by previous generations.[4] In this light we come to understand that the crisis in so-called religious literacy—the capacity of religious ways of thinking to enrich society—is part of a greater crisis in an educational system which has failed to play its role as a key link in a cultural chain. This is where we glimpse the broader dimensions of the *Progetto* as a reappraisal of the Church's mission in public life.

It is important to bear in mind that the Church's teaching on education goes far beyond an interest in the life, mission and structures of Catholic educational institutions. The Church sees authentic education as an indispensable foundation for a good society. Benedict's multiple references to an 'educational emergency' should not be understood solely as comment on a situation found in schools with a Catholic foundation. On the contrary, the 'educational emergency', so-called, is a manifestation of the broader challenge to 'authority' in society. This is not simply a questioning of the limits of government in daily life or a challenge to the workings of the legitimately-ordered functions of the state. The roots are deeper: the questioning of the human person's responsibility to act as an active agent in the transmission of key cultural values, whether in the family or in the school, is a rejection of the existence of a set of values which transcends personal choice. In this reading of affairs, there is no pre-determined right and wrong to which private and public life should be ordered:

> Educating, however, has never been an easy task and today seems to be becoming ever more difficult. Parents, teachers, priests and everyone who has direct educational responsibilities are well aware of this. Hence, there is talk of a great 'educational emergency', confirmed by the failures we encounter all too often in our efforts to form sound people who can cooperate with others and give their own lives meaning. Thus, it is natural to think of laying the blame on the new generations, as though children born today were different from those born in the past. There is also talk of a 'generation gap' which certainly exists and is making itself felt, but is the effect rather than the cause of the failure to transmit certainties and values.[5]

Benedict's comments merit further and deeper consideration. Of course, we could pose questions such as: on what grounds does he conclude that education is indeed in a state of emergency? Is this a universal phenomenon or is it confined to the educational systems of the industrialised west (the so-called 'first world')? Nonetheless, for the Catholic educator today, Benedict's words have to be set in the wider context of the contemporary drive towards utilitarianism and managerialism in educational systems.

Returning to Benedict's subtly radical statement above, he draws on his considerable experience as an academic to challenge the idea that young people today are essentially different to young people of past ages. His understanding of the 'generation gap' turns the accepted wisdom on its head: for Benedict, the 'gap' has arisen because of deficiencies in educational approaches which have left more than one generation bereft of the cultural legacy which is their right. This is not to say that there are not challenges facing young people which older generations did not face: as we argued above, technological advances have made knowledge easily accessible; the rise of virtual/online friendships have the potential to drive people to retreat behind the presumed safety of the keyboard; the availability of on-line shopping has minimised opportunities for human interaction in the market-place and the damage done by the easy availability of toxic substances is recognised universally. Alongside these pernicious phenomena, a diminution of respect for the sanctity of the body has lead to a cheapening of sexual identity with devastating social consequences in broken families. Despite these many and doubtless deep challenges, the Christian proposes that the young person, today as always, remains a child of God. He or she will benefit from authentic education in the virtues to allow them to live a good life and make a positive contribution to society through their work well done, a high level of cultural awareness and a recognition of the value of meaningful personal relationships.

Returning to the question of transferability, the *Progetto* is, clearly and unsurprisingly, marinated in the life, thought patterns and ecclesial realities of Italy. In a strict sense, such a local dimension is not transferable as a package. Such direct transferability might not be desirable in a Church which values the rooting of universal values in local contexts. For such a reason, the existence of a wide menu of local ecclesial initiatives in educational and cultural matters is a sign of the Church living out what Pope John Paul II has called a 'spirituality of communion'. Indeed the Synod of Bishops, while not a parliament of the Church, is one example of the theology of communion in that it is a manifestation of local churches gathering in prayer and dialogue with the Bishop of Rome, who is himself the guarantor of unity.

In referring to efforts to make the Church a reflection of this communion, the words of Pope John Paul II offer some further food for thought:

> Before making practical plans, we need *to promote a spirituality of communion,* making it the guiding principle of education wherever individuals and Christians are formed, wherever ministers of the altar, consecrated persons, and pastoral workers are trained, wherever families and communities are

> being built up. A spirituality of communion indicates above all the heart's contemplation of the mystery of the Trinity dwelling in us, and whose light we must also be able to see shining on the face of the brothers and sisters around us. A spirituality of communion also means an ability to think of our brothers and sisters in faith within the profound unity of the Mystical Body, and therefore as 'those who are a part of me'.[6]

It is clear, therefore, that the *progetto* is a localised reflection of the 'spirituality of communion'. It is more than the mere building of networks and partnerships, important as this is. Rather, it is a powerful initiative designed to develop the theologically-conditioned cultural depths of the Church in the context of a deep and meaningful dialogue with other expressions of culture. It reflects a desire to locate the Church's mission at the heart of national life and provide opportunities for the 'Catholic mind' to penetrate the world of ideas as expressed in literature, art, health care, politics and, of course, education.

Wider Church Initiatives

Our understanding of how Catholic education can be recognised as an engagement with culture will be enlarged when it is set beside three related initiatives in contemporary Catholicism: Year of Faith; New Evangelisation; Courtyard of the Gentiles.

Year of Faith

The *Year of Faith* (2012–2013) was a celebration of 50 years of Vatican II—itself a call to renew Catholicism's engagement with the 'spirit of the age'. The famed *aggiornamento* (updating) is not a reconstruction of the legacy of the Church's theological tradition but a fresh attempt to present the insights of the Catholic mind to a world in need of direction and guidance. The call in *Gaudium et Spes* for dialogue between the Church and other ways of thinking is an inspiration for the *Progetto*'s stated desire to place the Gospel at the heart of the public square. The *Year of Faith* offered the Church an opportunity to reflect on and develop its mission to evangelise.

New Evangelisation

The *New Evangelisation* is an overarching theme which supports a range of initiatives designed to address the marked decline of religious practice in the west. It recognises the effects of secularism and pluralism on the Church and does not deny the catechetical weaknesses which have beleaguered the Church in recent times. It seeks to strengthen and encourage a confident outreach to the peripheries of society in order to re-engage traditionally Christian nations with the message of the Gospel. It is not easy to gauge how the *New Evangelisation* will inform the life of the Church in the coming decades. If it is to be effective, it needs to move beyond rhetoric and aspiration and show that it is not simply about the counting of converts as an indicator of success.

The *Progetto* is not orientated primarily towards catechesis but its 'educational' angle emphasises the importance of authority and tradition in the life of the school; when applied to catechesis, these concepts call for a sustained and systematic teaching of doctrine in the Religious Education syllabus. This syllabus should be accessible to people of all religious traditions, and none.

Courtyard of the Gentiles

The *Courtyard of the Gentiles* is a curiously-named initiative designed to build bridges with atheism. It recalls the second Jewish Temple which had an outer court where the Gentiles were allowed to gather in order to have some form of association with the Jewish religious culture.[7] In Benedict's mind, the new understanding of 'Courtyard' is a form of outreach to those who seek a wider understanding of reality. He set out this vision in his 2009 address to the Roman Curia:

> I think that today too the Church should open a sort of *Courtyard of the Gentiles* in which people might in some way latch on to God, without knowing him and before gaining access to his mystery, at whose service the inner life of the Church stands. Today, in addition to interreligious dialogue, there should be a dialogue with those to whom religion is something foreign, to whom God is unknown and who nevertheless do not want to be left merely Godless, but rather to draw near to him, albeit as the Unknown.[8]

The *Courtyard of the Gentiles* is an innovative response to the Council's call to reach out to have dialogue with atheists.[9] A key means here is the promotion of public initiatives in the cities of Europe such as Bologna, Paris, Barcelona, Warsaw and Budapest.[10] What unites all these initiatives is a confidence in Catholicism's capacity to make a *positive* contribution to the common good. As such, they are manifestations of the Church's social teaching as applied to education and culture.

While the *Progetto* is clearly 'made in Italy', its articulation of the need to integrate the Catholic worldview in the culture serves as an invitation to the wider Church to engage seriously with the challenges the Church and modern society faces today. In looking ahead, we gain strength from our heritage and, in keeping with a truly Catholic spirit, seek to renew the Church by drawing on our many doctrinal and cultural sources.[11]

Catholic Education as the New Paideia

The *Progetto* is a prototype of the bold and confident moves towards the renewal of the Church's dialogue with culture which is part of the *Courtyard* initiative. Within the desire to engage in dialogue with all expressions of contemporary thought lies the question of the relationship between secular culture and religious faith: can we still say that dialogue can lead to the Truth? To answer this question satisfactorily, it is essential to look to and learn from the early Church's engagement with Greek philosophy and consider what this means for contemporary Catholic education.

Early Christian education emerged from the processes of Jewish education in which all education was 'religious education': a family-centred nurturing process which aimed to integrate the child into the faith tradition and cultural practices of the community.[12] The early Church's missionary impulses led it beyond the conceptual borders of Judaism to embrace a cultural milieu shaped by Greek language and civilization.[13] The eventual accommodation between the revealed religion of Christianity and Greek philosophy—sometimes known as the marriage between Jerusalem and Athens—formed a new conceptual framework for Christian education. The Church's absorption of the Greek notion of *paideia*—the formation of good people who will be ideal members of the *polis*—made Christianity the 'new philosophy': the Gospel is the answer to humanity's search for the true, the good, the beautiful. Thus from its very beginning, Catholic education, broadly understood, was far more than a moment of catechesis but encompassed a wider search for meaning which, without doubt, retained the core of Christianity but was not averse to philosophical dialogue. Some of the early Christian thinkers saw classical literature as types, or precursors, of Christian thinking. Their acceptance of the value of non-Christian thinking as a step towards the Truth is a valuable lesson for the contemporary Church's educational mission.[14]

One of the most helpful examples from history is the conversion story of St. Augustine of Hippo (354–430 AD). A strong case could be made for St Augustine as the first Catholic thinker to offer a well-worked rationale for Catholic education.[15] Augustine's life straddled the end of the fourth and the beginning of the fifth century. He was a witness to the demise of antiquity and not for nothing can his life and teaching be described as an axial point in Christian history. Augustine's path to Christianity has many sources, not least the prayers of his mother, St.

Monica. Although the young Augustine had been enrolled as a catechumen, he drifted from any substantial religious commitment in favour of the study of rhetoric. Augustine's conversion from teacher of rhetoric to lover of philosophy and then from lover of philosophy to Catholic Bishop and teacher of the Catholic faith are, for the believer, reflections of the working of grace within the interface of culture and academic life.

Augustine's conversion journey was initiated by his discovery of the *Hortensius* of Cicero. This book caused him to re-assess his career as a teacher of rhetoric. It opened his mind, at that time full of the pride which a glittering academic career offered, to a more profound awareness of the richness of philosophical contemplation:

> It was my ambition to be a good speaker for the unhallowed and inane purpose of gratifying human vanity. The prescribed course of study brought me to a work by an author named Cicero, whose writing nearly everyone admires, if not the spirit of it. The title of the book is *Hortensius* and it recommends the reader to study philosophy. It altered my outlook on life. It changed my prayers to you, O Lord, and provided me with new hopes and aspirations.[16]

This revelation changed the world of Augustine and in consequence, the trajectory of Christian history. In the world of antiquity, to enter the world of philosophy was more than a change of profession: it was a radical change of lifestyle. The 'philosophers' formed a community where the great questions of life were debated and reflected upon as a matter of course.[17] The search for truth served as the mood music of their common life.

The second spur to conversion was Augustine's encounter with the figure of St Ambrose, Bishop of Milan. Augustine catches sight of the Bishop as he (Ambrose) is reading quietly in his garden.[18] While this famous passage does not reveal which particular text or texts the Bishop was reading, it would be reasonable to suggest that he was studying a portion of Scripture in preparation for a sermon or an instruction to catechumens. Whatever the text was, the importance of this passage lies in the personification (in Ambrose) of the union of prayer and study, the heart and the intellect. This dynamic relation is at the heart of all attempts to understand and foster an authentic Catholic educational culture. It is a corrective to any religious or academic 'fanaticism' which would separate and set in opposition the concepts of faith and reason. Catholic institutions, to be sure, must be a site of the 'great discussion between faith and reason'.[19]

For Augustine, as for others, engagement with other ways of thinking paved the way for an eventual embrace of the Catholic faith. This is not to say that all study of such expressions of culture will necessarily lead to God. For Augustine, however, God's grace allowed him to navigate a safe passage through the contours of philosophy and come in time to knowledge of the Truth. Thus this committed engagement with the cultural expression of the age (the *saeculum*) brought him to knowledge of the Truth. In applying this to the modern age, the equivalent of the 'philosophy' of Augustine's time is the secularist mindset in which the creeds of relativism and personal fulfilment guide public life and influence and shape educational systems.[20] These ideals are constructed as beneficial for society at large and, in some cases, have corrected overly rigid interpretations, some would say misunderstandings, of Christianity. The correct Christian response to these challenges is crucial and must go beyond a harsh and hackneyed dismissal of those who hold these views. The better response is to reframe the debate as a way to build bridges with Christian ideals.[21] This approach would seem to offer a more fertile terrain for dialogue than the firing of random shots across a presumed ideological divide.

There are, of course, limitations to the Church's desire to engage with broader ideas. There is the constant risk of either too close an assimilation to contemporary cultural norms—leading to a dilution of a distinctive Catholic worldview—or an overly sharp reaction to the trends of secularism with the result that the Catholic intellectual tradition becomes an 'underground' movement which has seceded from all means of dialogue with the world.[22] Neither position is an accurate reflection of the Church's desire to engage fruitfully, and from a position of confidence, with the world. The way ahead is to refresh these traditional means of engagement and support them with new ways of working with the world of culture. In this endeavour, our key sources must be, in the first place, the Scriptures, the documents of Vatican II and the *Catechism of the Catholic Church*. The documentary legacy of the Popes who followed the Second Vatican Council are interpretive tools for the application of the Council's teaching in different social and cultural domains.

To conclude this section, the process of cultural transformation in schools begins by identifying what is of value in other and seemingly hostile ways of thinking. The very act of dialogue as proposed above is an expression of Catholic culture. It is one small but vital step in the renewal of the Catholic culture in education. There follow some practical indications of how this can be done.

Building a Catholic Culture in Schools

The liturgy is the key source of Catholic identity and hence of Catholic culture.[23] It is in the ever-deeper understanding of the rhythms of the liturgical year that the believer glimpses an authentic Catholic pedagogy woven within the succession of fasts, feasts, ritual and silence.

A truly nuanced understanding of liturgical renewal avoids, as Benedict XVI has reminded the Church, a hermeneutic of rupture and embraces a sense of continuity.[24] This allows the past to enrich the present and, in broad terms, offers a rich vision of the human person as made in *imago dei* but in need of grace in order to live a good life. The principles of continuity and organic growth can be usefully applied to the pedagogy and mode of operation of the Catholic school and allow the beauty, richness and depth of the liturgical year to underpin the life of the Catholic school.

To transform our Catholic schools into centres of a rich Catholic culture is no easy task. It requires a broader rethinking of our approaches to intellectual, cultural and religious formation. It is vital that local Churches study prayerfully the Magisterial corpus on education and culture: this body of teaching offers a rich diet of material for prayer, reflection and study. However, it is important not to underestimate the complexities arising from the sheer volume of information on education and culture available to us today from both Magisterial and other Catholic sources. This process of sifting and evaluating material is to be understood as more than a clearing process designed to find ideas which suit our own unique tastes. Rather, it assists our understanding of the layers of meaning contained in these key sources for education and, crucially, allows for flexibility and nuance in its local application. This is the heart of the Catholic school's mission to promote the transformation of culture: local Churches applying universal principles and thus demonstrating how subsidiarity informs practice.

The following *keys* are an attempt to open this field for further study and energise the institutions of Catholic education as centres of Catholic culture.

First Key: The Catholic University as Cradle and Guardian of Catholic Culture

Although the focus in the present volume is on the Catholic school, it is not possible to do justice to the matters at hand without some recognition of the place of the Catholic university in the life of the Church. The Catholic university or higher education institution, however denominated, has the unique opportunity to play a key local, national and international role in the shaping of ideas and the building of an academic climate which is unrestricted by the neuralgic demands of performativity allied to somewhat narrow definitions of what constitutes success. With Catholic anthropology at the heart of its teaching and research, the Catholic university should be encouraged to see itself as the 'guardian' of the original meaning of the university: to seek 'wisdom' and view all knowledge in a theological light. Its catholicity is not a narrowing of the range of experiences offered to the student body. Its desired academic and organisational excellence are welcome signs of the Church's commitment to the promotion of an 'authentic humanism' for our times, one which places Christ at the centre of humanity's quest for happiness.

In the secular university, the local Church has to take all the necessary steps to ensure that Catholic staff and students have satisfactory levels of pastoral support. A vibrant university chaplaincy provides a point of entry to the worldwide network of Catholic tertiary educational institutions, itself a sign of the communion of the Church. In addition, the doctrinal formation of academics should be a priority of the Bishop and the university chaplain: seminars, conferences and an organised programme of open lectures by the Bishop to academic staff would remind the wider community of the ecclesiastical origin of the European universities and, crucially, that the principles underpinning those origins remain of relevance today.

The formation of voluntary associations of Catholic academics from both Catholic and secular universities offers a form of synergy which should add value to the Catholic educational world's much-needed dialogue with wider academic and cultural ideas. This is where the Catholic university community can bring its gifts to bear on the 'Courtyard of the Gentiles' initiative and use the intellectual climate of the university and the chaplaincies to make a distinctive contribution to the life of their institutions.

Second Key: School, Curriculum and Culture

The broad curriculum of the Catholic school has to be shaped in line with Catholic thinking on education. While the school, as public institution, must operate within the legal and constitutional limits of lawful authorities, it should do so mindful of the Church's educational heritage and its potential to shape national systems. Authentic Catholic education, we argue, should be the richest experience of education.

Education needs, at the same time, to promote everything that is true, good and beautiful about the human person: that is to say, educate the mind and the emotions to appreciate reality.[25]

This appeal to what is 'true, good and beautiful' is a sign that Catholic education must look beyond viewing education as simply a training for future employment. Catholic education is a vector of evangelisation by means of its mission to offer a worthwhile and broad educational experience to all, regardless of faith tradition. In this approach Catholic education is inclusive while retaining a necessary and theologically-conditioned distinctiveness.

A key aspect of the curriculum in the Catholic school is that of 'order'. This is neither a synonym for academic regimentation nor any amalgam of small-minded attempts to impose uniformity on all aspects of the life of the school. Order as here proposed is a reflection of the divine plan for humanity: we are called to holiness and, in response to grace, are called to live good (or orderly) lives on earth.

The incarnation of 'order' in the curriculum configures the process of education as the gradual discovery of the will of God for each of us. To be happy is to have a soul which has accepted the order of providence and which finds genuine happiness therein. Referring to St Augustine, Kevane says:

> His thesis is clear: happiness is the health of the soul and this health of the soul depends upon the fare which the soul is given. The structure arranged in human affairs to feed the souls of men (sic) is the educational establishment.[26]

As such the purpose of a Catholic educational system is to allow the students to experience order in the life of the school, including in the curriculum, and to foster a balanced order in their own lives. This is given particular shape in the curriculum of studies offered. The Catholic school can offer a counter-cultural educational opportunity driven by the historically-conditioned Catholic approach to education. In a speech to Bishops of France, Benedict XVI had this to say about the purposes of education:

> As regards Catholic schools which have shaped the Christian and cultural life of your country, today they have a historical responsibility. As places for the transmission of knowledge and the formation of the person, of unconditional acceptance and of learning, these schools often enjoy a well-deserved status. It is necessary to find a way to ensure that the transmission of faith stays at the centre of the educational project.[27]

These words remind us that Catholic education holds to a view of education which some would call outdated in its commitment to 'transmission of knowledge'. In so doing, Catholic education is truly counter-cultural in its dedication to the need to conserve the best of the past while seeking new insights in the light of tradition across all academic subjects, not just in the field of Religious Education.[28]

Third Key: Institutes of Catholic Culture as Sources of Renewal

Alongside the university and the school, another important element of Catholic intellectual culture would be the formation of 'cultural centres'. Indeed such centres would be extensions of the Catholic educational system and would be an innovative way of placing the Church's artistic and intellectual patrimony at the heart of the plural society. How these institutions are shaped is a matter for localised decision-making; they would certainly offer a forum for Catholic educational bodies to unite with other Catholics and like-minded people to consider how the Catholic vision can enhance the common good of society. They would bring together the sense of outreach inherent in the Courtyard of the Gentiles with the pastoral energy surrounding the New Evangelisation. They would be closely linked to the Catholic school and university and would function closely with them. Indeed they would act as a resource for all Catholic educational agencies and for the wider mission of the Church.

In keeping with the idea of 'voluntary association' noted above, these centres would not necessarily originate with the local Bishop and the educational agencies of the Church. Of course, to be designated as 'Catholic' the approval of the Bishop is necessary. It is important that these centres are not categorised, implicitly or otherwise, as *museums* where venerable traditions are dusted down and admired as symbols of former ways of doing things. They would be places where the Catholic intellectual tradition and its artistic and cultural patrimony would be re-presented as fundamental sources of modern thought. Some practical examples illustrate how this could be done.

- Study sessions of Dante's *Divine Comedy* showing how the Catholic theological vision is woven through his peerless poetry (even in translation) and striking 'images'. This text (popularly known as the 'fifth' Gospel) has much to tell us about humanity's search for fulfilment as the sinner is guided from Hell, through Purgatory to Heaven.
- Courses in understanding Christian art as theology *without words*: this would explore how a deep understanding of sacred art will enhance our liturgy, faith formation and appreciation of beauty. The Internet has opened the doors of so many museums/galleries and churches that access to good art is within range of a keyboard. Nonetheless, these works are best appreciated within the liturgical and historical context: that is where the role of the tutor is indispensable.

- Performances of 'sacred music' would be accompanied by discussion of the theological rationale for the doctrine(s) considered in the piece. For example, the performance of a Requiem (Verdi/Fauré) would be preceded by a talk/discussion on the 'Four Last Things' and on why the Catholic Requiem Mass is not principally a celebration of the life of the deceased.
- Academic seminars on the distinctive Catholic contribution to the growth of mass education throughout the years: the monastic school, the universities and the important role of the Religious Orders, Societies and Congregations in the promotion of the education of women. This is a key theme in wider historical studies of education and has much to offer the contemporary Catholic community.

Fourth Key: Supporting Catholic Educators

The support given to the staff of the Catholic school is a sign of the Church's commitment to the quality and depth of the education provided in its schools. Francis encapsulated the necessity of such formation in an address to the Congregation for Catholic Education:

> The educator in Catholic schools must be, first of all, very competent, qualified and, at the same time, rich in humanity, capable of being in the midst of young people with a pedagogical style, to promote their human and spiritual growth. Young people are in need of quality teaching, together with values not just enunciated but witnessed. Coherence is an indispensable factor in the education of young people.[29]

While many local churches celebrate 'Catholic education week' and offer a menu of development initiatives, there is considerable scope for a more sustained approach in which a systematic study of the Catholic educational tradition would feature. This would involve courses in theology, the philosophy of education and models of leadership, for example.

The 2012 Synod of Bishops recognised the need for teachers to receive 'on-going formation in carrying out their responsibilities.[30] How can this be done? Some practical suggestions follow:

- In the first place, all teaching staff should be encouraged to attain Masters level qualifications, where possible. We need to consider if Head Teachers/School Principals should be encouraged to study at a higher level and to consider what benefits such endeavours would bring to the school.
- We must recognise the practical difficulties arising from asking professionally committed teachers to commit themselves to higher studies. This might require schools to be generous in allowing staff some (limited) access to sabbaticals in order to allow time for study. More broadly, Catholic universities and colleges which share in the mission of Catholic teacher education must seriously consider how they can support school staff by means of online modules and summer schools.
- The subjects studied by staff need not be wholly linked with professional practice: it is far more important that the staff model in their own studies the value of education as the search for wisdom and understanding. This approach would broaden the vision of the teacher and bring new insights to their practice. Professional learning, so-called, cannot be reduced to a set of utilitarian steps undertaken with an eye simply on career advancement. Education is a richer field and dialogue between *outcomes for professional learning* and 'education for wisdom' would be a

more fitting arrangement for those who operate within the field of Catholic education.

Concluding Remarks

In this chapter we have explored how the contemporary Catholic school can be conceptualised as a 'cultural project'. In presenting these arguments we recognise that the debate is only beginning. The enmeshing of Catholic school systems in the West within the culture of public education needs challenging: for example, Catholic schools, no matter their particular funding arrangements, must engage fully with state examination systems. Nonetheless, it is not sufficient to say that Catholic education is 'distinctive' while aligning our systems, to a greater or lesser extent, to models of education promoted by the state. We argue that Catholic schools will benefit from a more robust engagement with all who have an interest in education. This book is a contribution to this debate.

In the appendices, we see clearly how the importance of cultural dialogue is rapidly becoming one of the principal poles around which contemporary Catholic educational thought revolves. This marks a new phase in the life of the Catholic school as dialogue becomes an explicit and necessary component of its missions to evangelise, catechise and educate.

Notes

1 *La Sfida Educativa* (2009) *passim.*

2 The rich variety of representations of 'the teacher' in the arts and humanities is the main focus of a recent collection of studies: R. McCluskey and S. J. McKinney (Eds.), *How 'The Teacher' is presented in Literature, History, Religion and the Arts: Cross-Cultural Analyses of a Stereotype* (Lewiston-Queenston-Lampeter: The Edwin Mellen Press, 2013).

3 *La Sfida Educativa* p. 57.

4 *See the Preface to La Sfida Educativa (2009).*

5 Benedict XVI, *Letter to the Faithful of the Diocese and City of Rome on the Urgent Task of Educating Young People* (2008).

6 Pope John Paul II, *Novo millennio ineunte* (2001), 43.

7 See the *Jewish Encyclopedia* (online): Temple of Herod http://www.jewishencyclopedia.com/articles/14304-temple-of-herod.

8 Pope Benedict XVI *Address to the Members of the Roman Curia and Papal Representatives for the Traditional Exchange of Christmas Greetings* (2009).

9 R. Landry *Reconstructing the Courtyard of the Gentiles* (2011), available at: http://www.integratedcatholiclife.org/2011/04/reconstructing-the-courtyard-of-the-gentiles/

10 The website of the Courtyard of the Gentiles gives a wide range of information on the story, scope and aims of the initiative: http://www.cortiledeigentili.com/template/default.asp?i_menuID=39896.

11 See L. Franchi, The Catholic School as Courtyard of the Gentiles in *Journal of Catholic Education* (formerly known as *Catholic Education: A Journal of Inquiry and Practice*) (2014) pp. 56-76) for a critical overview of the link between Catholic education and the *Courtyard* initiative.

12 There are many interesting studies of this subject. See the following: C. Horn and J. Martens, *'Let the Little Children Come to Me'-Childhood and Children in Early Christianity* (Washington DC: Catholic University of America Press, 2009); W Strange, *Children in the Early Church* (Milton Keynes: Paternoster, 2006); M. Bunge (Ed.), *The Child in Christian Thought* (Cambridge: Eerdmans Publishing Company, 2001).

13 W. Jaeger, *Early Christianity and Greek Paideia* (London: Oxford University Press, 1961 / 1977) p. 5.

14 Clement of Alexandria, *Stromata* (ch. V) in A. Roberts and J. Donaldson (eds.), *Ante-Nicene Library-Translations of the Writings of the Fathers Down to AD 325* (Edinburgh: T & T Clark, 1867); Clement of Rome, *The First Epistle of Clement to the Corinthians* in A. Louth and M. Staniforth (Eds.), *Early Christian Writings* (London: Penguin, 1987).

15 R. Topping, *Happiness and Wisdom-Augustine's Early Theology of Education* (Washington DC: The Catholic University of America Press, 2012); E. Kevane, *Augustine the Educator* (Westminster Maryland: the Newman Press, 1964).

16 Saint Augustine, *Confessions*, III, 4.

17 P. Hadot, *Philosophy as a Way of Life* (Translated by Michael Chase) (Oxford: Blackwell Publishing, 2008); Topping *Happiness and Wisdom-Augustine's Early Theology of Education* (2012).

18 St. Augustine, *Confessions*, VI, 3.

19 Pope Benedict XVI, *Ad Limina to Bishops of France* (30 November 2012).

20 For a comprehensive critique of the influence of relativism on educational thought see J. Arthur, L. Gearon, A. Sears, *Education, Politics and Religion—Reconciling the Civil and the Sacred in Education* (2010).

21 *Catholic Voices* has encouraged Catholics to engage in a fruitful way with those who hold other views. Examples of this approach as applied to contemporary debates can be found in A. Ivereigh, *How to Defend the Faith Without Raising Your Voice* (Huntingdon IN: Our Sunday Visitor, 2012). See also the website of *Catholic Voices* http://www.catholicvoices.org.uk.

22 For more on this theme, see the address by Cardinal George Pell to the St. Andrew's Year of Faith Conference, *From Vatican II to the New Evangelisation*: http://www.xt3.com/library/view.php?id=11757.

23 *Catechism of the Catholic Church,* 1136f; Topping, *Happiness and Wisdom-Augustine's Early Theology of Education* (2012) chapter 3. The journal *Antiphon: A Journal for Liturgical Renewal,* a publication of the Society for Catholic Liturgy, is an important source for articles on this theme. http://www.liturgysociety.org.

24 Benedict XVI *Address to the Members of the Roman Curia and Papal Representatives for the Traditional Exchange of Christmas Greetings* (2009).

25 Synod of Bishops (2012) Proposition 27.

26 Kevane, *Augustine the Educator* (1964) p. 89.

27 Pope Benedict XVI *Ad Limina to French Bishops* (30 November 2012).

28 R. Davis and L. Franchi, 'A Catholic Curriculum for the 21st Century' in *International Studies in Catholic Education* vol. 5/1 (March 2013), p. 36–52.

29 Pope Francis, *Plenary Address to the Congregation for Catholic Education* (2014): See Appendix 2 of this volume.

30 Synod of Bishops (2012) Proposition 27.

AFTERWORD

CATHOLICISM, CULTURE, MODERNITY: A POST-SECULAR TURN?

Robert A. Davis

THE RECEPTION EXTENDED to Pope Francis by an international media simultaneously enthralled and bewildered by his elevation to the Chair of Peter was always bound to be one that educated Catholic opinion would view with some caution.[1] The obvious personal charm of the new Pope, alongside the authentic simplicity of his lifestyle and reticence of his public manner, clearly unsettled the organs of an establishment accustomed to containing figures of his stature and influence within the standard discourses of political celebrity on the one hand and detached, most irrelevant, hieratic authority on the other. Francis has clearly subverted both styles of media translation, commanding at least for the time being a quite distinctive mode of *moral* attention, which has unsettled some of the opponents of the Church while at the same time winning the Papacy a genuine global popularity with a generation weary of the threadbare geopolitical, cultural and economic reassurances of its own thoroughly compromised ruling elites. It is almost as if educated opinion in many parts of the world glimpses behind Francis's disarming smiles and everyday gestures of intimate warmth the restoration of an ethical wholeness which, while acknowledging the complexity and diversity of the modern age, dares to propose that the common humanity prized by activists of all faiths and none may be much more immediately tangible and realisable than our multiple ideological refractions of it have for a long time been suggesting to us. In an era of 'interventions'—humanitarian, environmental, infrastructural, even military—Francis signals that the most significant intervention is the interpersonal encounter with the alienated poor and, by implication, with the materially alienated elements of our own wounded and unfinished selves.[2]

Benedict XVI's heroically intellectual recovery of a European vision of civic, democratic wellbeing tested by the fires of history and trauma was similarly and daringly rooted in the assertion of *love*—for which he received much less credit than he merited—clearing the intellectual detritus of a century (or more) of shattered political obsessions and empty consumerist promises in order to reconnect the European imaginary with some of the lost sources of its cultural and spiritual vitality in the deepest narratives of a Continent-crossing Christendom.[3] This was a language that European opinion often found difficult to comprehend in Benedict's comparatively short papacy (and periodically scorned as institutional hypocrisy), for the reasons Benedict himself understood too well: the amnesia of an unfinished Enlightenment project in denial over some of its deepest self-contradictions and resolutely shunning the memories of its disastrous political failures and their complicity with those self-same rationalist and revolutionary values from out of which had sprung the darkness of state terror alongside the light of popular emancipation and knowledge.[4] It may be a central element of Benedict's legacy to have achieved exactly what he set out to do even before he became Pope: to reclaim a viable memory of Christendom not as a decadent imperial spectre stifling the spirit of individual liberty and collective feeling, nor as a nostalgic archival recollection, but as a living, vital source of critical self-examination, person-centred moral restraint and endless charitable absorption in the claims of the Other-foregrounding the flourishing of our neighbour as the ultimate measure of technological efficacy and civic liberation.

The combination of these historic forces—channeled through two men of outstanding individual character, perhaps, but fully representative of longer-term developments larger than both—has opened out a unique set of possibilities for a new kind of engagement with the evolving patterns of modernity and postmodernity at the heart of the Church's encounter with the contemporary world. Even before Francis took up his papacy, or Benedict challenged the centres of European opinion-formation, intellectual dissatisfaction with dominant yet exhausted post-war anti-religious paradigm had begun to express itself in the registers of global academic and journalistic debate.[5] This shift in the climate of enquiry had a number of direct causes and a likely shared origin in the continuing upheavals of late modern globalisation. The advance of liberal democratic values associated with the costly defeats of the totalitarian regimes of the 'short' twentieth century, and culminating in the resolution of the Cold War and the collapse of the Soviet Union in the early 1990s, carried at its heart a lengthy master-narrative of rational, Enlightened progress emblematised by overarching institutional innovations penetrating almost every aspect of day-to-day life in the seemingly triumphant West: the coming of the post-war welfare states; the emancipation of women; the decolonization of moribund maritime empires; the public funding of mass education from kindergarten to university; the victory of science, medicine and technology over the deadly politics of scarcity and the perpetual menace of implacable natural forces; the vindication of a kind of benevolent liberal market capitalism capable of sustaining apparently boundless economic growth and amenable to regulation in the interests of the prosperity and wellbeing of all.[6] Even when buffeted by periodic energy crises, or when overshadowed at key junctures by the sombre threat of further, devastating international conflict, this postwar democratic settlement proved remarkably resilient in convincing large sections of the world's population that a two-hundred-year movement of gradualist human improvement, momentarily and bloodily diverted by the last gasps of reactionary Old European hostilities, had been fully resumed and would in the course of time deliver the transformed civilization prophesied by the greatest of the *philosophes*.

As several critical commentators have observed, this vision of human flourishing was in its modern forms only rarely expressly anti-religious.[7] Certainly, it viewed ancient institutions such as Churches and monarchies as of essentially curatorial interest, and it implicitly invested its hopes in a post-religious understanding of individual and societal possibility. But in contrast to the dominant aggressive rhetoric of the *philosophes*, who were elevated of course as the movement's intellectual founders, prevailing forms of postwar optimism assumed a generally benign view of the legacy of European religious sentiment and its colonial and imperial offshoots. In part this was simple recognition of the scale of continuing religious adherence amongst the European population and the depth of influence of the major Catholic and Protestant congregations on the daily patterns of public life and private belief. It also quite probably reflected a habit of ongoing cultural respect for the Christian Churches as the custodians of certain traditions of European memory—increasingly eclipsed by the successor functions of the state, perhaps, and imprinted with the growing sense of intergenerational dissociation from the doctrinal expectations of the Churches, but nonetheless worthy of the reverence accruing to institutions in which were invested the heritage of Europe's medieval and antique past, including the theological sources from out of which the Continent's distinctive identity had been forged and preserved. As late as the closing years of 1950s, the deliberations of the major Lutheran congregations, or the announcement of an historic Ecumenical Council of the Roman Catholic Church, could be met with sincere attentiveness at the centres of European public opinion, even where the most important vehicles of communication no longer formally reflected a sanctioned ecclesial interest or ratification.[8]

As John Gray and others have claimed, a rubicon in altering this consensus was crossed in the 1960s, when a potent combination of forces stamped with the permissive and liberationist values of the era came to see consensus as collusion and lost patience with the backsliding, inertia and supposed hypocrisy of the modernising gradualists.[9] The coming to power and influence of younger men and women no longer shaped by the ethos of the liberal-Christian coalition that had seen off the menace of the 'pagan' dictators and that had steadily dismantled the faltering European empires, cast the Christian Churches in a role much more consistent with the adversarial stance of the radical anticlerical Enlighteners of the mid-18th century. An older oppositional register was reanimated, in which the Churches and their leaders were positioned as villainous reactionaries standing in the way of progress, reason and human rights. Christianity was to be condemned in this perspective as an outmoded guardian of obscurantism, hierarchy, superstition, oppression and denial, stifling the fulfillment of humanity's natural, embodied instincts and the shared human longing for freedom, whilst constraining the aspirations for political equality and economic participation of multiple excluded and marginal groups now demanding political voice.

As Arthur Marwick has shown, it was in this critical period that a remaking of the major institutions of European and American public life took place, installing at their heart a cadre of educated thinkers and activists whose values were indelibly secular in outlook and who were—to various degrees and in various dispositions—committed to the pervasive understanding that the religion of their forebears was inimical to progress and destined ultimately to wither before exposure to the forces of economic opportunity and social deliverance.[10] For thirty years, between 1965 and 1995, the influence of these groupings worked a powerful alchemy at the heart of democratic culture, capitalising upon an unprecedented period of affluence and extended social mobility which seemed to suggest that many of the underlying conditions of shortage, uncertainty and exclusion upon which deep-seated religious sentiment depended were to be forever banished from human concern by concerted political and economic action. In no area of social life was this more fully dramatized than in the processes of immigration that unfolded across the northern hemisphere in the 1960s and 70s as the old European empires dissolved and their previously colonised possessions came to be linked to their former imperial sovereignties by new kinds of economic relationship and exchange. Acceptance of large-scale labour migration from former colonies became one of the cornerstones of mid-twentieth century economic growth, on the firm progressivist assumption that immigrant populations from a vast spectrum of ethnicities and cultures would be readily assimilated into their host societies by the irresistible and homogenising forces of economic opportunity and educational integration.[11] Within this process, refractory cultural loyalties such as religious belonging would be incrementally abraded or worn away by prolonged exposure to education, wealth, pluralism and the manifest rationality of shared liberal values from which all would self-evidently be benefiting. A fundamental empiricist assumption of Enlightenment sociology would then be comprehensively vindicated and the long-forecast 'Death of God' would accelerate in the European homelands, henceforward seen as a beacon of secular and rational values. None of this would require coercion or inducement, it must be stressed, because it simply followed iron anthropological laws vouchsafed by Europe's own internal experience of social change, secularisation and the widespread abandonment of religious belief.[12]

Understanding how and why late modern Europe's story departed so markedly from this preordained and seemingly incontestable script is not easy, even if the paramount explanation is the most obvious one alluded to throughout this commentary: the complexities of globalisation. Anxiously oversimplified accounts in some quarters have pointed to one major world religion that either has not performed to type or whose subversion of the governing plotline exposes to view the narrative's underlying Eurocentric and racist assumptions. This is of course, Islam—Europe's perpetual 'other', in which resistance to post-imperial Weberian secularisation has proven most tenacious supposedly because of the great monotheistic faith's alternative configuration of the relationship of religion to society, law and individualism. In this account, the influx of Muslims into Europe as part of the 'third wave' of traditional immigration in the 1980s introduced into modern democratic culture a vibrant and productive minority fully compliant with the economic logic of migration and development (and even, within limits, civic participation) but unyieldingly committed to continuing religious particularism and fideistic obedience undiminished by the allures of secular material success. The endurance of Islamic difference both disclosed the patronising condescension of an essentially Eurocentric Judaeo-Christian ideology of progress *and* suggested that the secularisation hypothesis had run up against limiting conditions of applicability, where seemingly contradictory values could be inscribed at the heart of the same evolving communities.[13]

There remains, however, a fundamental inadequacy with even this explanation. Reliance on Islamic exceptionalism has not really survived the onrush of globalisation in the last twenty years, which far from confining continuing religious fidelity to besieged confessional pockets or beleaguered incomer bridgeheads has seen the encounter of the religious, the quasi-religious, the non-religious, the anti-religious and the 'spiritual' take on some quite unprecedentedly novel forms and styles of interaction.[14] In part this is attributable to the rise within the globalised movement of peoples of multiple and hybridised micro-populations of religious minorities from outwith the great monotheistic faith communities. In part, it is also derived from the now endless mixing and turbulence to which all such variegated groups—majorities and minorities—are subject as the technologies of global communication and exchange blur boundaries between groups and individuals, giving rise to fluid, striated and provisional identities. But it may go still further. Many thinkers have since the turn of the millennium argued that the apparent end of secular multiculturalism and the so-called 'return of religion' are in fact *effects* of globalisation itself—expressed both in the reassertion of the local, the indigenous and the particular in the face of functional economic anonymity *and* in the creation and proliferation of alternative networks of international solidarity at obvious variance with the attenuated logic of economic instrumentalism.[15] If this analysis is correct, then liberal democratic culture requires to address conditions of social and political existence far more nuanced and complex than its early champions had predicted, in which religion has not only unexpectedly 'returned' as an object of scholarly enquiry and civic salience, but where it quite probably never really disappeared in the first place.

This is not at all to deny the demographics of European secularisation and the haemorrhaging of members from some of the Continent's historic Churches and congregations. Nor is it to suggest that 'immigrant' religions have somehow found the secret of being distinctively modern and resolutely traditional at the same time. All religions are subject to the forces of change, realignment, decline and renewal and there is abundant evidence of the profiles of migrant faiths also shifting perceptibly over comparatively short periods of time. Undoubtedly, the processes of economic and social modernisation interact in extraordinarily subtle ways with the inner lives and allegiances of believers across the generations in a broad cross-section of faith communities. Nevertheless, the complexity of religious identity and belonging in contemporary European society, and the corresponding adjustments to the sociological and philosophical discourse in which this is discussed and examined, has called for a far-reaching refurbishment of the lexicon within which the encounter of the sacred, the profane, the secular and the spiritual is to be interpreted and interrogated.[16]

The notion of the 'post-religious' society has been variously pondered in recent times as one possible way forward from the present academic impasse. Philosophers such as Jurgen Habermas[17] and Peter Nynas[18] see it offering a viable heuristic for the necessary reconfiguration of religion and spirituality within the institutions of a European social-democratic order jolted by the seeming 'return of religion' in strains quite at odds with the orthodox Weberian conception of onward progressive rationality. Amongst the several weaknesses of the classically Weberian 'secularisation hypothesis' was of course its reliance on 'hard naturalism'. Another was its dependence on the 'teleological assumption' referenced above that religious affiliation intrinsically represents a 'pre-Enlightenment' condition of being destined gradually to atrophy in the face of higher (more ethically appropriate and compelling) forms of applied rationality vindicated by a supervening moral and political order. These weaknesses, several critics have suggested, give rise to naïve forms of occlusion and ignorance of the dialectic of influence that is increasingly manifest today in complex societies labouring under the conditions addressed by Francis and Benedict. Indeed, over the past decade and more, conceptions of *secularism and post-secularism* have replaced 'post-religious' at the heart of critical social theory and philosophy of religion largely because of the conditions so presciently described by Benedict and so startlingly addressed by Francis.[19]

With the older genre of 'ideology critique' fading, alongside its background theoretical logic of 'structural understanding' and neo-Marxism, and with contemporary intercultural politics correspondingly failing so far to make itself distinct in these regards from an exhausted generalised multiculturalism no longer in command of popular or electoral support, the enhanced salience of religious motivations, practices and modalities of belief has had to be reconsidered, to say the least, non-reductively in the public spaces of European Church and society.[20] Concomitantly, straight 'secularist' understandings of the course of (radical) modernity, in the terms of which religious identifications would progressively be replaced by some species of consolatory philosophico-scientific materialism—taking hold most especially in popular mores and in mass education—have at last fallen seriously into question. Or rather, the inherent reliance of radical forms of critique upon some such secularist scenario, even if only implicitly, has become more readily recognisable than previously—and increasingly regarded as unconvincing.

The resulting multiplication of post-secular dialectics has been extensive, with *postsecularism* perhaps best understood not as any kind of clearly-defined adversarial coalition acting in opposition or reproach of secularism, but as a shifting spectrum of concerns and possibilities and interpellations intended to awaken debate to a pressing social and cultural reality.[21] Hence interventions sited towards the 'religious' end of the post-secular spectrum would include not only Charles Taylor's outstanding reassertion of 'the way of transcendence' (to borrow Alister Kee's pregnant phrase[22]) in *A Secular Age*,[23] but also the intellectual energy and theological fertility visible in the project of radical orthodox theology as an exercise in critical theory and applied Christian anthropology.[24] In the Marxist secular-materialist position, by contrast, stands a maverick thinker such as Slavoj Zizek, who defends the Judaeo-Christian heritage in a kind of theatrically subversive 'strategic' or 'millenarian' fashion as a source of apocalyptic interruption in our degraded, unjust and politically complacent cultures,[25] alongside critical theorists such as Pierre Hadot[26] or Alain Badiou,[27] who hold unshakably to historicist philosophical principles, but whose high-octane populist vocabularies are nevertheless peppered with routine intimations of infinity, eternity, grace, mindfulness and the possibilities of personal and social transformation through the healing of the soul. Somewhere at the literary-critical edges of this spectrum sit John Caputo[28] and Gianna Vattimo,[29] engaging intently on the post-structuralist prospect of a revelation beyond the dialectics of theism; or Jonathan VanAntwerpen,[30] developing grounds for dialogue between 'naturalism and religion' which eschews the limitations of Habermas' liberal consensualism in favour of the motivational experience and inner alchemy of faith; and even the later 'Levinasian' reflections of the elderly Derrida, gesturing in the enigmatic sign-language of the post-Holocaust, post-structuralist rabbis towards a 'religion without/beyond religion'.[31]

For all the activity and volubility within this terrain, its habits of thought and enquiry now unmistakably incline away from the established and hitherto unassailable, totalising secularist perspectivism that gripped the institutions of European learning from the end of the 19th century onwards and on into the convulsions of the 20th. Recently, even politically and socially engaged theorists such as Terry Eagleton,[32] Peter Watson[33] and Roger Scruton[34] have from quite contrasting ideological outlooks proposed to relaunch the whole project of Western ethics on the basis of this massive, supertanker realignment of European habits of discovery, with religion reallotted a central, if perhaps not yet paramount, place in the styles of ethical and moral reasoning and contestation typical of social institutions such as universities and schools. In their cases, religion means Christianity, but postcolonial commentators have long argued that it is the compound Christian-secularist heritage of modern Western thought that prevents it from fully respecting religions like Islam, and from fully comprehending the anthropologies of those non-Western societies such as China that it then demarcates crudely as 'traditional' or 'hybrid'.

At the outset of his landmark study of more than a decade ago *Formations of the Secular*, Talal Asad set the terms of much post-secular polemic: 'What is the connection', he asked, 'between "the secular" as an epistemological category and "secularism" as a political doctrine?'[35]. His response then proceeded to articulate in academic terms the deep sense of popular unease repeatedly reflected in the barometers of 'mass observation'style public opinion analysis. In 'secular ideology', Asad and others suggested, the rich and diverse human practices of religion are reverse-engineered as matters of a dispossessed 'faith' and 'belief' attaching to specific sorts of discursively declassified ontological objects or spheres of meaning—most especially the difficult, troubling category known as the 'supernatural'. Here stand, as Inglehart has argued, many of the defining claims of the sacred—whether it be the existence of immortal souls, the call to prayer and submission or the ultimate destiny of the universe.[36] Secularism, by contrast, is uniquely determined by the instruments of a 'natural' understanding and with the consequent hegemonic conscription of shared cultural space as a zone regulated exclusively by the real-rational and the *social*, thereby annexing to itself the right to determine the ontological grounds for segregating the things of 'this world' from the claims of any supervening spiritual order of signs and symbols, powers and principalities impinging on this world.

Actualising these epistemological distinctions, a 'political metaphysic' can then be seen to dominate secular space, defining the 'transcendent' identity of the citizen at the heart of 'public' or 'national' life and collective decision-making, whilst simultaneously consigning the metaphysical vindications and longings of religion—their symbolic aura diminished and domesticated in the process—to the realm of the imagination and of personal, private recreational life. With this stigmatising binary then institutionalised in secular law, Asad insists, the role of the state, far from being genuinely 'tolerant', cannot be other than coercive and exclusionary, usurping to itself the consequential task of enforcing what counts as being truly human. Hence democratic liberalism—whilst affecting the protection of these same centuries-old ideals of neutrality and tolerance—

emerges from this appraisal not as the self-declared impartial arbiter but as the temporary victor in an ongoing battle for the maintenance of what William Cavanaugh, following Nietzsche, has defined ironically as its three 'religious' myths: the myth of the violent state as the rescue from violence; the myth of collusive civil society as free space; and the myth of dehumanizing economic globalization as authentic, achieved catholicity.[37] There is thus a necessary, palpable connection between epistemological, political and educational secularism, and a correspondingly inexorable tendency of the secular state towards symbolic and political violence in the operation of even its most inclusive and pluralised institutions. There is also a bitter irony: secularism requires and even reproduces 'religion' as its own discursive and political condition of existence.

Even in abbreviated form, Asad's argument is salutary for all those committed to pursuit of the goals of explanation and understanding that would appear to form part of the structures of power arbitration and knowledge legitimation that he so eloquently describes. In consequence, influential commentators like Jose Casanova[38] and William Connolly[39] have since amplified the *post-secular* as a means not only of systematically challenging 'the established unconscious of European culture', but also 'the secular self-understanding of modernity that is constitutive of the social sciences', including the philosophy and theory of education—because mass education, in the language of its classical Enlightenment rationale, is not simply an *effect* of secularisation, but its very *engine*. Hence in the dominant secularist educational logic of discovery, hypothesis and explanation, the apparently irrational is consistently re-presented in terms of real-rational containment, and the apparently transcendent is encoded into a 'this-worldly' discursive or aesthetic experience, courtesy of what Asad terms a kind of 'sociological truth'. The most routinely observed of these processes has been, of course, the persistent rebranding (or 'translation') within liberal educational practice of the past forty years and more of dangerous religious investment as safe, contained cultural performance.

It is, of course, always controversial to depict the objectification of faith as the product or consequence of exclusively secularist categories. Charles Taylor's main purpose in his own post-secularist assessment is to demonstrate—echoing Robert Markus before him[40]—that Christianity was profoundly and designedly implicated in the emergence of what we think of now as secular thinking. Asad also knows this of course, and adds richly to this essentially Augustinian story, but he still hints that because of this enabling relationship, Christianity might perhaps have to be thought of as a 'transgressive' or 'improper' religion in an almost Girardian sense, since it is the faith that has carried the germ of Western secularism inside its theological understanding of the polity all along. More substantively for the purposes of pluralist religious dialogue of the kind championed throughout this book, we need to consider that many religious people today, and by no means only Christians, seek inclusion and recognition in the 'secular' public sphere precisely on the grounds of their 'faith' and its claims upon that sphere, conceived in part in the 'epistemological' sense and in part as a moral obligation and a political imperative. Their 'faith', indeed, is what has defined their disposition towards shared social existence, and it is what they take to ground the moral distinction between themselves and other, complementary actors in the shared domain of justice and good work. So while we learn much from post-secularism's account of how, in past societies, faith was principally regarded as pertaining to the exercise of virtue rather than the avowed declaration of knowledge or belief, these discursive representations are inescapably more interwoven today into a complex lattice of consensus, permission, resistance and subversion—whether this is ultimately the 'product' or 'effect' of secularism or not. And it seems eccentric, as a consequence, to be suggesting today to believers that their understanding of their own faith would alter if only they could see that its presence in the public square is the secret charitable indulgence of its seeming opposite.

With this important philosophical qualification in mind, perhaps in the final reckoning, the main purpose of the critique of secularism of the last twenty years or so has been simply to constrain its more 'triumphalist' variants, underlining Asad's claim that the 'straightforward narrative of progress from the religious to the secular is no longer acceptable' and amplifying his 'skepticism about the way in which secularism and the secular are set within a progressivist story' inclining inveterately towards the demise of active religion in all but its residual, left-over forms of personal piety and social solidarity. The powerfully anti-secularist strain in William Connolly's writings, particularly his slowburner manifesto, *Why I Am Not a Secularist* of 1999, perhaps presses most insistently at the provisional boundaries or accommodations established by the likes of Taylor and Asad around the institutional practices and recuperative legitimising strategies of postmodern education and culture.

Connolly insists that the dichotomies that are thought to be typical of secular social learning and good judgement—public and private, reason and emotion, fact and value, the cerebrally cognitive and the instinctively visceral—have on the threshold of the globalising twenty-first century irretrievably broken down. Secularists, he further avers, uphold such distinctions prophylactically mainly in order arbitrarily to ward off any dangerous 'metaphysics of the supersensible' and what it might entail for their working scientific paradigms. In other words, these contrasts themselves stand, precisely, as foundational metaphysical commitments. Viewed in this light, exclusively secular philosophies can be regarded, and indeed must be pitied, Connolly daringly suggests, as essentially 'winter' doctrines, formulae in search of an impossible moral stabilisation and purified cognitive integrity found nowhere in the lives of living, breathing citizens or the structures and 'forms of life' through which they are brought to political and religious consciousness. If instead we cultivate in our learning and our enquiries what he terms an 'impious reverence for life', embracing rather than eschewing our yearnings for the intangible, the transcendent, the chthonic and the impure—and if we wholeheartedly accept the authentic hybridity of the modes of apprehension through which we grasp uncertainly the 'protean energies' of desire that flow through the organisation of being, then we are better placed to avoid the political and symbolic exclusionism that necessarily results whenever the 'irrational' or the 'religious' is intellectually traduced or scientifically stigmatised. The result of this recalibration of our spiritual senses is the affirmation of a genuinely pluralistic, life-enhancing ethical commitment, Connolly argues, radicalised beyond the confines set even by Taylor—one that requires us to renounce altogether the traditional juxtaposition of sceptical social science and orthodox quizzical pedagogy against the demands of religious world-views. 'Multiple loyalties' might then seriously be nurtured throughout our cultural and educational systems—a receptive spiritual disposition that is nothing less than the very soul of the 'democratic adventure' in a plural and diverse civilisation.

For the living traditions of Catholic study and reflection, there is nothing but invitation in the post-secular landscape. The schools, universities, research institutes, monasteries, apostolic fraternities, retreat centres, lay associations through which contemporary Catholic opinion is fostered and nourished in the midst of great ideological turmoil, stand already at multiple crossroads on the pilgrim-routes of the European mind and the encounters with otherness with which it has been shaped. They are, as both Benedict and Francis, have appreciated, heirs to a struggle for humanity as well as a celebration of it; custodians of diverse and dynamic habits of thought and argument fully accustomed to the scrutiny of rival and even antipathetic world views, extending hospitality and inclusion to all who are prepared to debate the future of humanity in a spirit of openness and dialogue. As the high tide of passing philosophical aberrations such as the so-called 'New Atheism' pass, their etiolated fundamentalism and bad manners alienating even the most 'Enlightened' mainstream political and social thinkers, the traditions of Catholic critical reflection seek no special privileges or exemptions, require no prior concessions for their entry into the public intellectual and deliberative spaces.

The respect extended to the very fact of participation in the civic conversation does not blunt critique, nor does it protect the Church from necessary accountability for past misjudgment or internal ethical failure. But the focus of the dialogue remains: a sustained examination of the multiple millennial challenges confronting the world and at the root of which lies a profound malaise, a confusion, a paralysis even before the understanding of the human person and the nature of the human person's flourishing and fulfilment. Whether this and related concerns are to be arbitrated ultimately by the reality of a loving God made known in revealed religion; by a humanity illumined by the lights of critical, secular rationality alone; or (as some insist) even by the distant and dimly-perceived promise of a post-human or transhuman utopianism at the edges of perception—the quest remains to apply the best of humanity's wisdom and insight to all of the monumental tasks before us.

Notes

1. P. Vallely, *Pope Francis: Untying the Knots* (London: Bloomsbury, 2013).
2. S. Von Kempis & P. E Lawler, *A Call to Serve* (London: SPCK, 2013).
3. P. Seewald, *Light of the World: The Pope, the Church and the Signs of the Times* (London: CTS, 2010).
4. A. O'Mahoney, 'The Vatican and Europe: Political Theology and Ecclesiology in Papal Statements from Pius XII to Benedict XVI' in *International journal for the Study of the Christian Church* 9/3 (2009), pp. 177–194.

5 H-G Ziebertz and U. Riegel, 'Europe: A Post-secular Society?' in *International Journal of Practical Theology* 13/2 (2009), pp. 293–308.

6 A. Phillips, *War, Religion and Empire* (Cambridge: CUP, 2011).

7 M. Burleigh, *Sacred Causes: Religion and Politics from the European Dictators to Al Qaeda* (London: HarperCollins, 2006).

8 C. Brown and M. Snape (Eds), *Secularisation in the Christian World* (London: Ashgate, 2010).

9 J. Gray, *The Silence of Animals: On Progress and Other Modern Myths* (London: Allen Lane, 2013).

10 A. Marwick, *The Sixties: Cultural Revolution in Britain, France, Italy and the United States, c.1958–c.1974* (Oxford: OUP, 1998).

11 R. Hansen, 'Migration to Europe since 1945: Its History and its Lessons' in *The Political Quarterly* 74/1 (2003), pp. 25–38.

12 A. Kundnani, 'Multiculturalism and its discontents: Left, Right and liberal' in *European Journal of Cultural Studies* 15/2 (2012), pp. 155–166.

13 T. Modood, 'Moderate Secularism, Religion as Identity and Respect for Religion' in *The Political Quarterly* 81/1 (2010), pp. 4–14.

14 N. G. Schiller, 'Localized neoliberalism, multiculturalism and global religion: exploring the agency of migrants and city boosters' in *Economy and Society* 40/2 (2011), pp. 211–238.

15 S. Kamat and B. Mathew, 'Religion, education and the politics of recognition: a critique and a counter-proposal' in *Comparative Education* 46/3 (2010), pp. 359–376.

16 D. Godzdecka *et al.*, 'From multiculturalism to post-multiculturalism: Trends and paradoxes' in *Journal of Sociology* 50/1 (2014), pp. 51–64.

17 J. Habermas, *Beyond Naturalism and Religion* (Cambridge: Polity Press, 2008).

18 P. Nynas *et al*, *Post-Secular Society* (New Brunswick, NJ: Transaction Publishers, 2012).

19 M. Sharpe and D. Nickelson (Eds), *Secularisations and Their Debates: Perspectives on the Return of Religion in the Contemporary West* (Dordrecht: Springer, 2014).

20 M. Wlevlorka, 'Multiculturalism: A Concept to be Redefined and Certainly Not Replaced by the Extremely Vague Term of Interculturalism' in *Journal of Intercultural Studies* 33/2 (2012), pp. 225–231.

21 G. McLennan, 'The Post-secular Turn' in *Theory, Culture, Society* 27/4 (2010), pp. 3–30.

22 A. Kee, *The Way of Transcendence: Christian Faith without Belief in God* (Harmondsworth: Penguin, 1971).

23 C. Taylor, *A Secular Age* (Cambridge, MA: Harvard University/Belknap Press, 2007).

24 J. Milbank and S. Oliver, *The Radical Orthodoxy Reader* (London: Routledge, 2009).

25 S. Zizek, *The Fragile Absolute: Or Why is the Christian Legacy Worth Fighting For?* (London: Verso, 2009).

26 P. Hadot, *Philosophy as a Way of Life: Spiritual Exercises from Socrates to Foucault* (Oxford: Wiley-Blackwell, 1995).

27 A. Badiou, *Second Manifesto for Philosophy* (London: Polity Press, 2011).

28 J. Caputo, *Truth: Philosophy in Transit* (London: Penguin, 2013).

29 G. Vattimo, *A Farewell to Truth* (New York: Columbia University Press, 2013).

30 C. Calhoun et al., *Rethinking Secularism* (Oxford: OUP, 2011).

31 J. Derrida, *Acts of Religion* (London: Routledge, 2002).

32 T. Eagleton, *Culture and the Death of God* (New Haven, CT: Yale University Press, 2014).

33 P. Watson, *The Age of Nothing: How We Have Sought to Live Since the Death of God* (London: Weidenfeld and Nicolson, 2014).

34 R. Scruton, *The Soul of the World* (Princeton, NJ: Princeton University Press).

35 T. Asad, *Formations of the Secular: Christianity, Islam, Modernity* (Palo Alto, CA: Stanford University Press, 2003).

36 P. Norris and R. Inglehart, *Sacred and Secular: Religion and Politics Worldwide* (Cambridge: CUP).

37 W. T. Cavanaugh, *Theopolitical Imagination: Discovering the Liturgy as a Political Act in an Age of Global Consumerism.* (London: T. & T. Clark, 2002).

38 J. Casanova, 'Secularization Revisited', in D. Scott and C. Hirschkind (eds), *Powers of the Secular Modern: Talal Asad and his Interlocutors* (Palo Alto, CA: Stanford University Press, 2006).

39 W. E. Connolly, *Why I Am Not a Secularist* (Minneapolis: Minnesota University Press, 1999).

40 R. A. Markus, *Christianity and the Secular* (Bloomimgton, IN: Indiana University Press, 2006).

APPENDIX 1

Congregation for Catholic Education

Educating to Intercultural Dialogue in Catholic Schools. Living in Harmony for a Civilization of Love

Introduction

It is a fact that today's society has a multicultural make-up, accentuated by globalization. The overlapping presence of different cultures is a great resource, as long as the encounter between those different cultures is seen as a source of mutual enrichment. However, significant problems can arise if multicultural society is seen as a threat to social cohesion, or as a threat to the protection and exercise of rights pertaining to individuals or groups. It is not easy to balance and harmonize previously established cultures and new cultures, as the two often demonstrate usages and customs that are mutually opposed. For some time now, multicultural society has been an object of concern for both governments and international organizations. In the Church, too, institutions and organizations of education and study, on both the international level and on national and local levels, have started to study the phenomenon and undertake specific projects in the field.

Education contains a central challenge for the future: to allow various cultural expressions[1] to co-exist and to promote dialogue so as to foster a peaceful society. These aims are achieved in various stages: (1) discovering the multicultural nature of one's own situation; (2) overcoming prejudices by living and working in harmony; and (3) educating oneself "by means of the other" to a global vision and a sense of citizenship. Fostering encounters between different people helps to create mutual understanding, although it ought not to mean a loss of one's own identity. Schools have a great responsibility in this field, called as they are to develop intercultural dialogue in their pedagogical vision. This is a difficult goal, not easy to achieve, and yet it is necessary. Education, by its nature, requires both openness to other cultures, without the loss of one's own identity, and an acceptance of the other person, to avoid the risk of a limited culture, closed in on itself. Therefore, through their experience of school and study, young people must acquire theoretical and practical tools for amassing greater knowledge both of others and of themselves, as well as greater knowledge of the values both of their own culture and of other cultures. They can achieve this by open-mindedly comparing cultures. In this way, they will be helped to understand differences in a way that does not breed conflict, but allows those differences to become opportunities for mutual enrichment, leading to harmony. This is the context in which Catholic schools are called to give their contribution, drawing on their pedagogical and cultural traditions, and in light of their sound pedagogical vision. Attention to the intercultural aspect of life is not new to the tradition of Catholic schools, as these are used to accepting students coming from various cultural and religious backgrounds. However, what is required in this field today is courageous and innovative fidelity to one's own pedagogical vision.[2] This is true wherever Catholic schools are found, both in countries where the Catholic community is a minority and in countries where the tradition of Catholicism is more rooted. In the former, one needs the ability to witness and dialogue, without falling into the trap of that facile relativism which holds that all religions are the same and are merely manifestations of an Absolute that no-one can truly know. In the latter group of countries, what is important is to give answers to the many young people "without a religious home", the result of an ever more secularized society.

The Congregation for Catholic Education remains faithful to the task entrusted to it after the Second Vatican Council: to deepen the principles of Catholic education. Hence, the Congregation wishes to offer its own contribution to encouraging and guiding education, in schools and Catholic educational institutions, along the path to intercultural dialogue. Therefore, this document is primarily aimed at: (1) parents, who have the first and natural responsibility for the education of their children, as well as organizations that represent families in schools; (2) head teachers, teachers and other personnel in Catholic schools who, together with the students, make up the educational community; and (3) national and diocesan episcopal commissions, as well as religious institutes, bishops, ecclesial movements, associations of the faithful, and other organizations that exercise pastoral care for education. We are also pleased to offer this document as a means of dialogue and reflection to all who are concerned for the education of the whole person, for the building up of a peaceful society marked by solidarity.

CHAPTER I

BACKGROUND

Culture and Plurality of Cultures

1. Culture is the particular expression of human beings, their specific way of being and organizing their presence in the world. Using the resources of their cultural heritage, which they possess from the moment of their birth, people can thus develop in a serene and balanced way, in a healthy relationship with their environment and with other human beings. Their ties with their own culture are necessary and vital; yet these ties do not force people into closing in on themselves in a self-referential way. In fact, people's cultural links are entirely compatible with encountering and knowing other cultures. Indeed, cultural differences are a

richness, to be understood as expressions of the human race's fundamental unity.

2. Globalization is one of the epochal phenomena of our time, and one which particularly touches upon the world of culture. It has shown the plurality of cultures that characterizes human experience, and facilitates communication among various areas of the world, involving all facets of life. This is not just something theoretical or general: in fact, every individual is constantly affected by information and news that arrive, in real time, from every corner of the world. He or she encounters, in everyday life, a variety of cultures, and thus experiences an increasing sense of belonging to what can be called the "global village".

3. Yet, this great variety of cultures is no proof for pre-existing ancestral divisions. Rather, it is the result of a continuous mixing of populations, denoted as the "mixed-race" factor, or "hybridization" of the human family in the course of its history. This means that there is no such thing as a "pure" culture. Different conditions of environment, history and society have introduced wide diversity within the one human community, in which, however, "each individual man is truly a person. His is a nature that is endowed with intelligence and free will. As such he has rights and duties, which together flow as a direct consequence from his nature. These rights and duties are universal and inviolable, and therefore altogether inalienable."[3]

4. The current phenomenon of multiculturism, bound up with the advent of globalization, today risks accentuating, in problematic ways, the "diversity in unity" that characterizes people's cultural outlook. In fact, the ever closer encounter between various cultures, in itself a dynamic process, creates much ambivalence. On the one hand, there is a push towards various forms of greater cultural uniformity. On the other hand, the specific nature of different cultures is exalted. One wonders what will be the fate of the specific identity of each culture, given the pressures of human migration, mass communication, the internet, social

networks and, above all, the enormous expansion of customs and products resulting in a "westernization" of the world. However, although this inexorable tendency to cultural uniformity remains strong, there are also many elements, alive and active, of variation and distinction between groups. These often provoke reactions of fundamentalism and self-referential closing in on oneself. Thus, pluralism and the variety of traditions, customs and languages—which of their nature produce mutual enrichment and development—can lead to an exaggeration of individual identity, flaring up in clashes and conflicts.

5. Yet, it would be wrong to hold that ethnic and cultural differences are the cause of all the many conflicts that disturb the world. In truth, these conflicts have political, economic, ethnic, religious and territorial causes; and are certainly not exclusively, or primarily, cultural conflicts. However, cultural, historical and symbolic elements are used to stir people up, to the point of encouraging violence rooted in elements of economic competition, social contrasts and political absolutism.

6. The ever increasingly multicultural nature of society and the risk that, contrary to their true nature, cultures themselves may be used as elements of antagonism and conflict are reasons for encouraging even more the build-up of profound intercultural relationships among both individuals and groups. In this light, schools are privileged places for intercultural dialogue.

Culture and Religion

7. Another aspect to be considered is the relationship between culture and religion. "Culture is broader than religion. According to one concept religion can be said to represent the transcendent dimension of culture and in a certain way its soul. Religions have certainly contributed to the progress of culture and the construction of a more humane society."[4] Religion is incultured, and culture becomes fertile ground for a richer humanity that measures up to its specific and profound vocation to be open to others

and to God. Therefore, "it is time ... to understand in a more profound way that the generating nucleus of every authentic culture is constituted by its approach to the mystery of God, in whom alone does a social order centred on the dignity and responsibility of the human person find its unshakeable foundation."[5]

8. In general, religion presents itself as the meaningful answer to the fundamental questions posed by men and women: "Men expect from the various religions answers to the unsolved riddles of the human condition, which today, even as in former times, deeply stir the hearts of men."[6] This characteristic of religions demands that they dialogue not only among themselves, but also with the various forms of atheistic, or non-religious, interpretations of the human person and history, since these latter are also faced with the same questions about meaning. Today, states and civil society, too, see how fundamental is the need for interreligious dialogue—meaning the broadest exchange among both individuals and communities, each with a different viewpoint. To avoid facile reductions and distortions in this sensitive field, it is opportune to highlight the following considerations.

9. Western society, which is ever more marked by multiculturalism, has an accelerating process of secularization, with the danger of an extreme marginalization of religious experience, seen as only being legitimate within the private sphere. More generally, in the dominant mindset, the anthropological question is quietly eliminated, i.e. the question about the full dignity and destiny of human beings. Thus, the aim is pursued of eradicating from culture all religious expression. However, awareness is lacking of how precious the religious dimension is for fruitful, proficient intercultural dialogue. In addition to this general mindset, there are other notable phenomena that also risk undervaluing the importance for culture of the religious experience. One can think of the spread of sects and of New Age, the latter being so much identified with modern culture that it is almost no longer considered a novelty.[7]

10. Religion emphasizes ultimate and definitive truths and, therefore, truths that lie at the basis of meaning, from which the prevalent Western culture seems to be distanced. In any case, religion is a decisive contribution to the building up of social community, in respect for the common good and with the intention of promoting every human being. Therefore, those who wield political power are called to judge carefully the possibilities for emancipation and universal inclusion demonstrated and effected by each culture and each religion. An important criterion for such evaluation is the effective capacity that the religions have for showing the worth of the whole person and of all people. Christianity, the religion of *God with a human face*,[8] carries a similar criterion within itself.

11. Religion can make its contribution to intercultural dialogue *"only if God has a place in the public realm."*[9] "Denying the right to profess one's religion in public and the right to bring the truths of faith to bear upon public life has negative consequences for true development. The exclusion of religion from the public square — and, at the other extreme, religious fundamentalism — hinders an encounter between persons and their collaboration for the progress of humanity. Public life is sapped of its motivation and politics takes on a domineering and aggressive character. Human rights risk being ignored either because they are robbed of their transcendent foundation or because personal freedom is not acknowledged. Secularism and fundamentalism exclude the possibility of fruitful dialogue and effective cooperation between reason and religious faith. *Reason always stands in need of being purified by faith*: this also holds true for political reason, which must not consider itself omnipotent. For its part, *religion always needs to be purified by reason* in order to show its authentically human face. Any breach in this dialogue comes only at an enormous price to human development."[10] Faith and reason, therefore, must recognize each other and enrich each other.

12. In the dialogue between culture and religions, due weight must be given to the discussion between faith and the various forms of atheism and non-religious humanist viewpoints. At the centre of this discussion must be the search for whatever favours the integral development of the whole person and of all people, without becoming bogged down in a sterile partisan clash. It also needs society to recognize the individual's right to his or her own identity. The Church, for her part, with the love that draws from the sources of the Gospel, following the pattern of the mystery of the Word's Incarnation, will continue to "proclaim that man deserves honour and love for himself and must be respected in his dignity. Thus, brothers must learn again to call each other brothers, to respect each other, to understand each other, so that man himself can survive and grow in dignity, in freedom and in honour. The more he suffocates the dialogue of cultures, the more the modern world is caught up in conflicts that risk being lethal for the future of the human civilization. Beyond prejudices, cultural barriers, divisions of race, language, religion and ideology, men must recognize each other as brothers and sisters, accepting each other in their diversity."[11]

The Catholic Religion and Other Religions

13. It is within this context that the dialogue among the various religions takes on a particular shape. It has its own profile, and particularly emphasizes the expertise of each religion's authorities. Naturally, interreligious dialogue, situated within the religious dimension of culture, touches upon some aspects of intercultural education—though not all, since the two things are not identical.

Globalization has increased the interdependence of peoples, with their different traditions and religions. In this regard, there are those who affirm that differences are by their nature causes of division and, therefore, at the most to be tolerated. Others even believe that religions should simply be silenced. "Rather, [differences] provide a wonderful opportunity for people of different religions to live together in profound respect, esteem and appreciation, encouraging one another in the ways of God." [12]

In this regard, the Catholic Church feels that the need for dialogue is ever more important. Such a dialogue, starting from an awareness of one's own faith identity, can help people to enter into contact with other religions. Dialogue means not just talking, but includes all beneficial and constructive interreligious relationships, with both individuals and communities of other beliefs, thus arriving at mutual understanding.[13]

Dialogue with both individuals and communities of other religions is motivated by the fact that we are all creatures of God. God is at work in every human being who, through reason, has perceived the mystery of God and recognizes universal values. Moreover, dialogue finds its *raison d'être* in searching for the patrimony of common ethical values found within the different religious traditions. In this way, believers can contribute to affirming the common good, justice and peace. Therefore, "since many are quick to point out the readily apparent differences between religions, as believers or religious persons we are presented with the challenge to proclaim with clarity what we share in common." [14]

Furthermore, the dialogue cultivated by the Catholic Church with other churches and Christian communities does not stop at what we have in common, but tends towards the highest goal of rediscovering lost unity.[15] Ecumenism has as its goal the visible unity of Christians, for which Jesus prayed for his disciples: *Ut omnes unum sint,* that they may all be one (*Jn* 17: 21).

14. There are various ways that believers can dialogue: there is the dialogue of life, with its sharing of joys and sorrows; the dialogue of works, collaborating to promote the development of men and women; theological dialogue, when this is possible, with the study of each other's religious heritage; and the dialogue of religious experience.

15. However, this dialogue is not a compromise, but rather a framework for reciprocal witnessing among believers who

belong to different religions. In this way, one gets to know the other's religion more deeply and better, as well as the ethical behaviours that derive from it. From direct and objective knowledge of the other person, and of the religious and ethical expectations that derive from his or her religious beliefs and practice, grow respect and reciprocal esteem, mutual understanding, trust and friendship. "In order to be true, this dialogue must be clear, avoiding relativism and syncretism, while at the same time it must be marked by sincere respect for others and by a spirit of reconciliation and fraternity."[16]

16. Clarity in dialogue means especially faithfulness to one's own Christian identity. "Christianity proposes Jesus of Nazareth. He, we believe, is the eternal *Logos* who became flesh in order to reconcile man to God and reveal the underlying reason of all things. It is he whom we bring to the forum of interreligious dialogue. The ardent desire to follow in his footsteps spurs Christians to open their minds and hearts in dialogue (cf. *Lk* 10:25-37; *Jn* 4:7-26)."[17] The Catholic Church proclaims that "Jesus Christ has a significance and a value for the human race and its history, which are unique and singular, proper to him alone, exclusive, universal, and absolute. Jesus is, in fact, the Word of God made man for the salvation of all."[18] Therefore, this being the indispensable condition for interreligious dialogue, it is also the indispensable condition for adequate intercultural education which is not divorced from one's own religious identity.

17. Catholic schools and institutes of higher education are important places for this education. What marks an educational institution as being "Catholic" is its addressing the Christian concept of reality, "its Catholic quality, namely its reference to a Christian concept of life centred on Jesus Christ."[19] Therefore, "Catholic schools are at one and the same time places of evangelization, well-rounded education, inculturation and initiation to the dialogue of life among young people of different religions and social backgrounds."[20] Pope Francis, addressing an Albanian

school, which "after the long years of repression of religious institutions, resumed its activity in 1994, accepting and educating Catholic, Orthodox and Muslim children as well as several pupils born into agnostic milieus", declared that "the school is thus becoming a place for dialogue and serene exchanges to encourage attitudes of respect, listening, friendship and a spirit of collaboration."[21]

18. In this context, "education must make students aware of their own roots and provide points of reference which allow them to define their own personal place in the world."[22] All children and young people must have the same possibilities for arriving at the *knowledge of their own religion* as well as of elements that characterize other religions. The knowledge of other ways of thinking and believing conquers fears and enriches ways of thinking about the other person and his or her spiritual traditions. Therefore, teachers are duty-bound always to respect the human person who seeks the truth of his or her own being, as well as to appreciate and spread the great cultural traditions that are open to the transcendent and that articulate the desire for freedom and truth.

19. This *knowledge* is not sufficient in itself, but *opens up to dialogue*. The more abundant the knowledge, the more it can sustain dialogue and co-existence with people who profess other religions. In the context of as open dialogue among cultures, different religions can and must make a decisive contribution to forming an awareness of common values.

20. In turn, *dialogue*, the fruit of knowledge, must be cultivated for people *to co-exist and build up a civilization of love*. It is not a matter of playing down the truth, but of realizing the aim of education which "has a particular role to play in building a more united and peaceful world. It can help to affirm that integral humanism, open to life's ethical and religious dimension, which appreciates the importance of understanding and showing esteem for other cultures and the spiritual values present in them."[23] Within intercultural

education, this dialogue aims "to eliminate tensions and conflicts, and potential confrontations by a better understanding among the various religious cultures of any given region. It may contribute to purifying cultures from any dehumanizing elements, and thus be an agent of transformation. It can also help to uphold certain traditional cultural values which are under threat from modernity and the levelling down which indiscriminate internationalization may bring with it."[24] "Dialogue is very important for our own maturity, because in confronting another person, confronting other cultures, and also confronting other religions in the right way, we grow; we develop and mature ... This dialogue is what creates peace", affirmed Pope Francis.[25]

CHAPTER II

APPROACHES TO PLURALISM

Different Interpretations

21. Pluralism is a plain fact in today's world. The question, then, is to evaluate dialogue's potential, as well as the potential within the integration of different cultures. The path of dialogue becomes possible and fruitful when based on the awareness of each individual's dignity and of the unity of all people in a common humanity, with the aim of sharing and building up together a common destiny.[26] Furthermore, the situation of the world today, as well as every culture's vocation, means choosing intercultural dialogue as a guiding concept, open to the future, when faced with the various interpretations of pluralism advanced and put into effect in society, politics and (with regard to our field of interest) education.

The reality of pluralism has been answered by two principal approaches: relativism and assimilation. Both are incomplete, though each has helpful points.

The Relativistic Approach

22. Being aware of the relative nature of cultures and opting for relativism are two profoundly different things. To recognize that reality is historical and changeable does not necessarily lead to a relativistic approach. Relativism, on the other hand, respects differences, but also separates them out into autonomous spheres, considering them as isolated and impermeable and making dialogue impossible. Relativistic "neutrality", in fact, endorses the absolute nature of every culture within its own sphere, and impedes the use of metacultural critical judgement, which would otherwise allow for universal interpretations. The relativistic model is founded on the value of tolerance, but limits itself to accepting the other person, excluding the possibility of dialogue and recognition of each other in mutual transformation. Such an idea of tolerance, in fact, leads to a substantially passive meaning of relationship with whoever has a different culture. It does not demand that one take an interest in the needs and sufferings of others, nor that their reasons may be heard; there is no self-comparison with their values, and even less sense of developing love for them.

23. An approach of this kind is at the basis of the political and social model of *multiculturalism.* This model offers no adequate solutions for co-existence, and fails to encourage true intercultural dialogue. "First, one may observe a *cultural eclecticism* that is often assumed uncritically: cultures are simply placed alongside one another and viewed as substantially equivalent and interchangeable. This easily yields to a relativism that does not serve true intercultural dialogue; on the social plane, cultural relativism has the effect that cultural groups coexist side by side, but remain separate, with no authentic dialogue and therefore with no true integration."[27]

The Assimilation Approach

24. What is called the assimilation approach is certainly no more satisfying. Rather than indifference towards the other culture, this approach is characterized by the demand for

the other person to adapt. An example would be when, in a country with mass immigration, the presence of the *foreigner* is accepted only on the condition that he renounce his identity and cultural roots so as to embrace those of the receiving country. In educational models based on assimilation, the *other person* must abandon his cultural references, to take on those of another group or of the receiving country. Exchange is reduced to the mere insertion of minority cultures in the majority one, with little or no attention to the other person's culture of origin.

25. More generally, the assimilation approach is advanced by a culture with universal pretensions, which seeks to impose its own cultural values by means of its economic, commercial, military and cultural influence. Here the danger is evident: "that of *cultural levelling* and indiscriminate acceptance of types of conduct and life-styles."[28]

The Intercultural Approach

26. Even the international community recognizes that the traditional approaches to dealing with cultural barriers in our society have shown themselves to be ineffective. Yet, how to overcome the barriers raised by positions incapable of giving a good interpretation to the multicultural factor? Opting for the logic of intercultural dialogue means not limiting oneself to strategies for the functional insertion of immigrants into the majority culture, nor to compensatory measures of a special nature. Indeed, it must be considered that the problem is not just one arising from immigration emergencies, but is the consequence of increased human mobility.

27. In fact, in a meaningful educational perspective, "today the possibilities of *interaction between cultures* have increased significantly, giving rise to new openings for intercultural dialogue: a dialogue that, if it is to be effective, has to set out from a deep-seated knowledge of the specific identity of the various dialogue partners."[29] From this point of view, diversity ceases to be seen as a problem. Instead, a community characterized by pluralism is seen as a resource, a chance for opening up the whole system to all differences

of origin, relationships between men and women, social status and educational history.

28. This approach is based on a dynamic idea of culture, which neither is closed in on itself nor celebrates diversity with stereotypes or folkloristic representations. Intercultural strategies function when they avoid separating individuals into autonomous and impermeable cultural spheres; they rather should promote encounter, dialogue and mutual transformation, so as to allow people to co-exist and deal with possible conflict. In summary, the goal is to construct a new intercultural approach, which aims at realizing an integration of cultures in mutual recognition.

CHAPTER III

SOME FOUNDATIONS FOR AN INTERCULTURAL APPROACH

The Teaching of the Church

29. The intercultural aspect is undoubtedly part of the heritage of Christianity, which has a "universal" vocation. In fact, in the history of Christianity there is the thread of dialogue with the world, in the search for greater fraternity among people. In the tradition of the Church, the intercultural perspective is not limited to appreciating differences, but helps to build up mankind's peaceful co-existence. This is particularly necessary in complex societies, where the risks of relativism and cultural uniformity must be overcome.

30. Numerous Church teachings, especially in the Second Vatican Council and in subsequent Magisterium, have reflected on *culture* and its importance for the complete development of human potential.

The Second Vatican Council, in considering the importance of culture, asserted that there is no truly human experience without the context of a specific culture. In fact, "man comes to a true and full humanity only through culture."[30] Every culture is a way of giving expression to the transcendental aspect of life; this includes reflection on the mystery of the world and, in particular, on the mystery of humanity. The essential meaning of culture consists "in the fact that it is a characteristic of human life as such. Man lives a truly human life thanks to culture. Human life is culture in the sense also that man is marked out and differentiated by it from all that exists elsewhere in the visible world: man cannot exist outside of culture. Man always lives in accordance with a culture that belongs to him and which, in turn, creates among men a bond that is also proper to them, determining the inter-human and social character of human existence."[31]

31. Moreover, the term *culture* indicates all those means by which "man develops and perfects his many bodily and spiritual qualities; he strives by his knowledge and his labour, to bring the world itself under his control. He renders social life more human both in the family and the civic community, through improvement of customs and institutions. Throughout the course of time he expresses, communicates and conserves in his works, great spiritual experiences and desires, that they might be of advantage to the progress of many, even of the whole human family."[32] Therefore, this includes both the *subjective* aspect—behaviours, values and traditions that each person takes on—and the *objective* aspect, that is, the works of individuals.

32. Consequently, "culture has necessarily a historical and social aspect and ... often assumes a sociological and ethnological sense. According to this sense we speak of a *plurality of cultures*. Different styles of life and multiple scales of values arise from the diverse manner of using things, of labouring, of expressing oneself, of practicing religion, of forming customs, of establishing laws and juridic institutions, of cultivating the sciences, the arts and beauty. Thus the customs handed down to it form the patrimony proper to each human community. It is also in this way that there is formed the definite, historical milieu which enfolds the man of every nation and age and from which he draws the values which permit him to promote civilization."[33]

Cultures show their nature to be profoundly dynamic and historical; they undergo changes in time. Nevertheless, beneath their more superficial changes, they show significant common elements. "Cultural diversity should therefore be understood within the broader horizon of the unity of the human race", in the light of which one can grasp the profound meaning of the very differences, instead of "the radicalization of identity which makes cultures resistant to any beneficial influence from outside." [34]

33. Therefore, *intercultural relations* are born not out of a static idea of culture, but of its openness. It is above all the potential *universality* of every culture that establishes dialogue among cultures.[35] Consequently, "dialogue between cultures … emerges as an intrinsic demand of human nature itself, as well as of culture … based upon the recognition that there are values which are common to all cultures because they are rooted in the nature of the person … It is necessary to foster people's awareness of these shared values, in order to nurture that intrinsically universal cultural 'soil' which makes for fruitful and constructive dialogue."[36] The openness to higher values common to the entire human race—based on truth and, moreover, universal, such as justice, peace, the dignity of the human person, openness to the transcendent, freedom of conscience and of religion—implies an idea of culture as being a contribution to a broader awareness of humanity. This is opposed to the tendency existing in the history of cultures, to build particular little worlds that are closed and introverted.

Theological Foundations

34. Defining human beings through their relationships with other human beings and with nature does not offer a complete answer to the unavoidable, fundamental question: *who is man really?* Christian anthropology places the basis of men and women and their ability to create culture in their being created in the image and likeness of God, a Trinity of Persons in communion. In fact, the patient pedagogy of God has been revealed to us from the very creation of the world.

Throughout salvation history, God educates his people to covenant—that is, to a living relationship—and to open themselves ever more to all peoples. This covenant has its high-point in Jesus, who, by means of his death and resurrection, has made it "new and eternal". From that moment, the Holy Spirit continues to teach the mission that Christ has entrusted to his Church: "Go therefore and make disciples of all nations … teaching them to observe all that I have commanded you" (*Mt* 28:19-20).

"Every human being is called to communion because of his nature which is created in the image and likeness of God (cf. *Gen* 1:26-27). Therefore, within the sphere of biblical anthropology, man is not an isolated individual, but a *person*: a being who is essentially relational. The communion to which man is called always involves a double dimension, that is to say vertical (communion with God) and horizontal (communion with people). It is fundamental that communion be acknowledged as a gift of God, as the fruit of the divine initiative fulfilled in the Easter mystery." [37]

35. The vertical axis of the individual's communion with God is authentically realized by following the Way that is Jesus Christ. In fact, "only in the mystery of the incarnate Word does the mystery of man take on light … Christ … fully reveals man to man himself and makes his supreme calling clear."[38] At the same time, this vertical axis grows in the Church which is "in Christ like a sacrament or as a sign and instrument both of a very closely knit union with God and of the unity of the whole human race."[39] "With the richness of the salvation wrought by Christ, the walls separating the different cultures collapsed. God's promise in Christ now became a universal offer … extended to all as a heritage from which each might freely draw. From their different locations and traditions all are called in Christ to share in the unity of the family of God's children."[40]

36. The horizontal axis of communion, to which men and women are called, is realized in interpersonal relationships.[41] Personal identity matures to the extent that people

live such relationships in an authentic manner. Relationships with other people and with God are, therefore, fundamental, because through them men and women increase their own worth. Relationships among peoples, too, among cultures and among nations strengthen and enhance those who enter into relationship. In fact, "the human community does not absorb the individual, annihilating his autonomy, as happens in the various forms of totalitarianism, but rather values him all the more because the relation between *individual and community* is a relation between one totality and another. Just as a family does not submerge the identities of its individual members, just as the Church rejoices in each new creation (*Gal* 6:15; *2 Cor* 5:17) incorporated by Baptism into her living Body, so too the unity of the human family does not submerge the identities of individuals, peoples and cultures, but makes them more transparent to each other and links them more closely in their legitimate diversity."[42]

37. The experience of intercultural relationships, just like human development, is profoundly understood only in light of the inclusion of individuals and peoples in the *one human family,* founded on solidarity and on the fundamental values of justice and peace. "This perspective is illuminated in a striking way by the relationship between the Persons of the Trinity within the one divine Substance. The Trinity is absolute unity insofar as the three divine Persons are pure relationality. The reciprocal transparency among the divine Persons is total and the bond between each of them complete, since they constitute a unique and absolute unity. God desires to incorporate us into this reality of communion as well: 'that they may be one even as we are one' (*Jn* 17:22). The Church is a sign and instrument of this unity. Relationships between human beings throughout history cannot but be enriched by reference to this divine model. In particular, *in the light of the revealed mystery of the Trinity,* we understand that true openness does not mean loss of individual identity but profound interpenetration."[43] The basis that Christian

tradition gives to the unity of the human race is found primarily in a metaphysical and theological interpretation of the "*humanum*" in which *relationality* is an essential element.[44]

Anthropological Foundations

38. The authentically intercultural dimension can be pursued due to its anthropological foundation. In fact, the encounter with another always happens between two flesh-and-blood individuals. Cultures take on life and continually redraw themselves starting from the encounter with the other person. To go out from oneself and consider the world from a different point of view is not a denial of oneself, but, on the contrary, is necessary for enhancing one's own identity. In other words, interdependency and globalization among peoples and cultures must be centred on the human person. The end of last century's ideologies, just like the spread today of ideologies that are closed to transcendent and religious reality, show how strong is the need to bring back central-stage the question about man and cultures. One cannot deny that men and women of our age, although progressing in many fields, have greater difficulty in defining who they are. The Second Vatican Council very well described this situation: "About himself [man] has expressed, and continues to express, many divergent and even contradictory opinions. In these he often exalts himself as the absolute measure of all things or debases himself to the point of despair. The result is doubt and anxiety."[45] The most significant indicator of this loss is the loneliness of men and women today. "One of the deepest forms of poverty a person can experience is isolation. If we look closely at other kinds of poverty, including material forms, we see that they are born from isolation, from not being loved or from difficulties in being able to love. Poverty is often produced by a rejection of God's love, by man's basic and tragic tendency to close in on himself, thinking himself to be self-sufficient or merely an insignificant and ephemeral fact, a 'stranger' in a random universe. Man is alienated when he is alone, when he is detached

from reality, when he stops thinking and believing in a foundation. All of humanity is alienated when too much trust is placed in merely human projects, ideologies and false utopias. Today humanity appears much more interactive than in the past: this shared sense of being close to one another must be transformed into true communion. *The development of peoples depends, above all, on a recognition that the human race is a single family* working together in true communion, not simply a group of subjects who happen to live side by side."[46]

39. Therefore, in order to establish intercultural relationships correctly, there needs to be a sound anthropological foundation. This latter must take as its starting-point the fact that human beings are, in their most intimate nature, *relational beings,* who can neither live nor develop their potential without being in relationship with others. Men and women are not just individuals, like self-sufficient monads, but are open and grow towards that which is different from them. Man is a person, a being in relationship, who understands himself in relationship with others. Moreover, his relationships arrive at their most profound level if they are based on love. Every individual aspires to love so as to feel fully realized, both in the love received and the capacity to give love in return. "Man cannot live without love. He remains a being that is incomprehensible for himself, his life is senseless, if love is not revealed to him, if he does not encounter love, if he does not experience it and make it his own, if he does not participate intimately in it ... In this dimension man finds again the greatness, dignity and value that belong to his humanity."[47]

40. The idea of love, in different forms, has accompanied the history of the various cultures. In ancient Greece, the most frequently used term was *eros,* love as passion, associated in general with sensual desire. Also used were the terms *philia,* often understood as love as friendship, and *agape,* to designate a high esteem towards the thing or person loved. The Biblical and Christian tradition under-

lines the oblative aspect of love. Yet, over and beyond these distinctions, there is a profound unity in diversity within the reality of love, which impels people to "an ongoing exodus out of the closed inward-looking self towards its liberation through self-giving, and thus towards authentic self-discovery and indeed the discovery of God." [48]

41. Love, when freed from egoism, is the way *par excellence* to fraternity and reciprocal help towards perfection among people. Love is an irrepressible desire, inscribed into the nature of every man and woman on earth. Not to receive love leads perforce to a lack of meaning and to desperation, and can lead to destructive behaviours. Love is the individual's true nobility, above and beyond his or her belonging to any culture, ethnic group, social stratum or position. It is the strongest, most authentic and most desired bond, which unites people among each other and makes them able to listen to each other, to pay attention to each other and to give other people the esteem they deserve. One can say that love is the method and goal of life itself. It is the true treasure, sought and witnessed to, in various ways and in various contexts, by thinkers, saints, people of faith and charismatic figures who, throughout the centuries, have been living examples of self-sacrifice as the sublime and necessary path to spiritual and social change and renewal.

Pedagogical Foundations

42. The above-mentioned theological and anthropological foundations lay sound foundations for an authentic intercultural pedagogy, which, by its very nature, cannot be separated from an understanding of man as person. Therefore, it is primarily not cultures but persons who enter into contact with each other—persons who are rooted in their own history and relationships. Hence, understanding interpersonal relationships is the basic pedagogical paradigm, both the means and the end for developing the person's very identity. This paradigm guides the idea of dialogue, ensuring that it is neither abstract nor ideological, but rather marked by respect, understanding and mutual service. It is then

nourished by the idea of culture as situated in history and dynamic, refusing to push the other person into a sort of cultural prison. Finally, it is aware that the relative nature of cultures is not the same as relativism; the latter, while respecting differences, simultaneously separates them into autonomous cosmoses, considering them as isolated and impermeable. Rather, our paradigm seeks, by every means, to foster a culture of dialogue, of understanding and mutual transformation, so as to reach the common good.

43. From this perspective, the understanding of intercultural relationships is neither differentialistic nor relativistic. Rather, it considers cultures as inserted into the moral order, within which the fundamental value is primarily the human person. Recognizing this basic fact allows people of different cultural universes who come into contact with each other to overcome their initial feelings of strangeness. This is not just a matter of mutual respect: the process implies that the subjects question their preconceptions, and that everyone understand and discuss the other's point of view.

44. From a pedagogical point of view, to develop such a difficult theme requires the courage and effort to become ever more aware of this complex and essentially multicultural reality. In particular, the discussion must be put into different words, so as to seek more intensely and more broadly for a common idea of education. Indeed, one seeks an idea of education to intercultural dialogue, understood as the individual's journey towards what must be, with a view to dialogue and mutual life-long learning.

CHAPTER IV

CATHOLIC EDUCATION IN VIEW OF INTERCULTURAL DIALOGUE

The Contribution of Catholic Education

45. The idea of cultures in dialogue is the light guiding the necessarily shared effort to overcome division. Within a frame-

work of mutual learning, one must know how to enter into the practical details of the dialectic that is provoked by some of the basic categories of life and culture ("clash/encounter", "closure/openness", "monologue/dialogue", etc.).

In this educational process, the search for peaceful and enriching co-existence must be anchored in the broadest understanding of the human being. This must be marked by a continual search for self-transcendence, seen not just as a psychological and cultural effort to supersede all forms of egocentricism and ethnocentricism, but also as spiritual and religious fervour, in harmony with an understanding of integral and transcendent development, of both the individual and society.

46. Therefore, communities that draw their inspiration from the values of the Catholic faith (families, schools, groups, youth organizations, etc.) must give voice and reality to an education truly based around the human person, in line with Christian humanist culture and tradition. There must be new commitment to the individual seen as "person in communion" and a new sense of his or her belonging to society. Otherwise, a looked-for society of free and equal individuals undoubtedly hides the risk of limitless, uncontrolled conflict and ambiguity.

Furthermore, the crucial link among individuals that together make up a society or community "requires a *deeper critical evaluation of the category of relation*. This is a task that cannot be undertaken by the social sciences alone, insofar as the contribution of disciplines such as metaphysics and theology is needed if man's transcendent dignity is to be properly understood." [49]

In light of the Trinitarian mystery of God, interpersonal relationships must be seen not just in their processes of communication; instead, like Love, they are the fundamental law of Being. This love is not generic, indistinct and merely tied to emotions; nor is it simply bound up with convenience or the rules of give-and-take. Rather, it is "free", as strong and generous as the love with which Jesus

Christ loved. In this sense, love is the will to "promote"; it is trust in the other person and, consequently, is a fundamentally educational act.

47. The concept of "love" in education directly implies those of "gift" and "reciprocity", which are fundamental aspects of education itself. Schools, both students and teachers, families and the wider community should promote that two-directional, to-and-fro movement which is love. We could thus summarize in outline the two movements: from love received to love given. Here, reciprocity is understood not simply in its final result, as equality of outcome, but primarily as a proactive step taken by the educator, whose vocation is to be the first to love.

These concepts will have to be examined again courageously, so as to further a pedagogy of communion. The goal is an educational ideal that moves educators to be credible witnesses in the eyes of young people. Reflection must follow on the crucial, strategic link binding "love of education" with "education to love". These two ideas are essential and indivisibly linked to each other. In them, both the educator and the student look towards the good, towards respect and dialogue.

Presence in Schools

48. John Paul II stressed this idea, and saw in the spirituality of communion[50] the most important challenge to be addressed in culture, everyday life, the family, at school and in the Church.

Before all other practical initiatives, there must be a spirit of unity that lives among individuals and groups. This is the perspective in which every value finds its foundation. It is the vital element forming the basis of all others. This is not just a spiritual challenge but also a cultural one, for all men and women of good will. Therefore, Catholic educators, teachers and students who find themselves in any type of school, who are united in the same art of love, must also take up this invitation.

49. Consequently, it is not the law by itself or any juridical form that builds up a community and keeps it alive. Rather, the spirit of the law creates active and responsible citizens, precisely in the measure in which the law is at the service of the common good and puts everyone in a condition of reciprocity. Therefore, a community's identity is mature to the extent that it takes on and continually and faithfully seeks to renew the values of co-operation and solidarity.
50. Schools are entrusted with great responsibility for intercultural education. During their formation, students find themselves interacting with different cultures, and need necessary tools for understanding them and relating them to their own culture. Schools are to be open to encountering other cultures. They have the task of supporting individuals so that each person develops his or her own identity in an awareness of its richness and cultural tradition. From the pedagogical and intercultural points of view, the finest gift that Catholic education can make to a school is that of witness. Catholic schools give witness to a constant, personal network of relationships, which are lived out between the poles of personal identity and otherness. This network is marked by dynamic osmosis, in the various dealings between adults (teachers, parents, educators, those in charge of institutions, etc.), between teachers and students, and among students—without prejudices of culture, sex, social class or religion.

Where Freedom of Education is Denied

51. In many areas of the world, for political or cultural reasons, it is not always possible to have Catholic schools. Sometimes, the Catholic presence is very limited and faces hostility. The issue is not merely one about claiming a right, the right to freedom of teaching and of schooling, but needs to be expressed in terms of a cultural offering that makes everyone richer. Therefore, one must ask: what can Catholic education offer in these situations?
Fundamentally, one must start by recognizing in others the same desire that is to be found in many religions and

cultures, in the important precept called the golden rule of humanity: "Do unto others as you would have them do unto you; do not do unto others what you would not have them do unto you". This is a moral law and is absolutely essential for social living. Love must be offered to all. This is the source of a new civilization, of humanity's true humanization, and is the opposite of all egoistic instincts to violence and war.[51]

52. This is the newness of education that flows also from Christian pedagogy, whose basis is to be found in the words of Jesus: "may they all be one" (*Jn* 17: 21). In fact, it shows the heart of all Christianity, the bearer of the mystery of God, who is Being in relationship, pure act of love. Here is found the newness of the Gospel, whose full acceptance implies, certainly, the faith, but whose effects transform the meaning of any encounter between individuals, groups, cultures and institutions.

53. Only this spirit of the search for unity can hold together the social order. This is solidarity in its totality, in every sense (religious, political, social, economic and professional). This is the alternative to that state of permanent rivalry which condemns people to be ever more incommunicado, even though they live in a globalized world—which condemns them to a increasing indifference both to the God proclaimed by Christianity and to any form of the Absolute. Therefore, young people are robbed of culture and faith, of their true meaning and of a suitable goal for which to strive. Thus, they risk dehumanizing life itself, in various ways. In these many "frontier" situations, where faith is daily put to the test, going against the current is often today, more than it has ever been, the Gospel choice. The pinnacle, the greatest gift, is the gift of oneself, giving one's life for others wherever justice and truth are violated.

54. Hence, in these very different contexts (atheism, fundamentalism, relativism, secularism), the "priority of value" must be placed back at the centre. This is principally a coherent witnessing; the gift of self; the capacity for seeking

and granting forgiveness, not out of exhibitionism or false moralising, but "for love", to assist in the world's development.

There exists an "important anthropological fact: the desire, which is proper to the human person, to have others share in one's own goods. The acceptance of the Good News in faith is thus dynamically ordered to such a communication," especially with those who "are lacking a tremendous benefit in this world: to know the true face of God and the friendship of Jesus Christ, God-with-us. Indeed 'there is nothing more beautiful than to be surprised by the Gospel, by the encounter with Christ. There is nothing more beautiful than to know him and to speak to others of our friendship with him'."[52]

CHAPTER V

THE CONTRIBUTION OF CATHOLIC SCHOOLS

Responsibility of Catholic Schools

55. In today's social context, demands are placed on Catholic schools in relation to the specific contribution that they can offer. Yet, this is not an easy task: indeed, it is facing ever greater obstacles. Catholic schools are seeing an ever growing presence of students with different nationalities and religious beliefs. In many countries of the world, most students profess a non-Catholic religion and the theme of interreligious encounter is now unavoidable. To avoid closing in upon "identity" as a goal in itself, educational pedagogy must take into account the growing multireligious component of society, with the consequent need to know about different beliefs and dialogue both with those beliefs and with non-believers.

56. It is important for Catholic schools to be aware of the risks that arise should they lose sight of the reasons why they exist. That can happen, for example, when they

unthinkingly conform to the expectations of a society marked by the values of individualism and competition. It can also happen through bureaucratic formalism, the consumerist demands of families, or the unbridled search for external approval. Catholic schools are called to give dutiful witness, by their pedagogy that is clearly inspired by the Gospel—*a fortiori* in a culture that demands that schools be neutral and removes all religious references from the field of education.[53] Catholic schools, being Catholic, are not limited to a vague Christian inspiration or one based on human values. They have the responsibility for offering Catholic students, over and above a sound knowledge of religion, the possibility to grow in personal closeness to Christ in the Church. In fact, "one of the fundamental human rights, also with reference to international peace, is the right of individuals and communities to religious freedom ... It is becoming increasingly important to promote this right not only from the negative point of view, as *freedom from*—for example, obligations or limitations involving the freedom to choose one's religion—but also from the positive point of view, in its various expressions, as *freedom for*—for example, bearing witness to one's religion, making its teachings known, engaging in activities in the educational, benevolent and charitable fields which permit the practice of religious precepts, and existing and acting as social bodies structured in accordance with the proper doctrinal principles and institutional ends of each."[54]

57. Catholic schools' primary responsibility is one of witness.[55] In the various situations created by different cultures, the Christian presence must be shown and made clear, that is, it must be visible, tangible and conscious. Today, due to the advanced process of secularization, Catholic schools find themselves in a missionary situation, even in countries with an ancient Christian tradition. The contribution that Catholicism can make to education and to intercultural dialogue is in their reference to the centrality of the human person, who has his or her constitutive

element in relationships with others. Catholic schools have in Jesus Christ the basis of their anthropological and pedagogical paradigm; they must practise the "grammar of dialogue", not as a technical expedient, but as a profound way of relating to others. Catholic schools must reflect on their own identity, because that which they can give is primarily that which they are.[56]

The Educational Community as an Experience of Intercultural Relationships

58. The model that school structures must take as their inspiration is the *educating community,* a place of differences living together in harmony.[57] The school community is a place for encounter and promoting participation. It dialogues with the family, which is the primary community to which the students that attend school belong. The school must respect the family's culture. It must listen carefully to the needs that it finds and the expectations that are directed towards it. In this way, the school can be considered a true experience of intercultural relationships, lived out rather than just spoken about.

59. Neutral societies and schools, which lack reference values and are uninvolved with any moral formation, do not develop participation. Nor, at the other extreme, does participation develop in societies or schools permeated by fundamentalist viewpoints. Rather, it flourishes in a climate of dialogue and mutual respect, in an educational setting where all are assured of being able to increase their capacities to the full, with the constant aim of pursuing the good of all. In this way, a constant climate of mutual trust, availability, of listening and of fruitful exchange can be developed, which must characterize the whole period of formation. Classes, which aim to give expression both to life and thought, are geared to creating a constant dialogue between teachers and students; enhancing the personal contribution of students in the common search for knowl-

edge; and giving rise to interdisciplinary teaching, with the contribution of teachers of various disciplines.

60. In schools, understood as educational communities, families have a most important place and role. Catholic schools appreciate their value, and promote their participation in the school, where they can assume various forms of co-responsibility. Even given that some families live in difficult circumstances and there are parents who do not follow the school's recommendations, families are always considered an indispensable reference-point, as bearers of appreciable resources. "Partnership between a Catholic school and the families of the students must continue and be strengthened: not simply to be able to deal with academic problems that may arise, but rather so that the educational goals of the school can be achieved."[58]

Educational Programme for Education to Intercultural Dialogue

61. The education offered by Catholic schools flows from their witness to the Gospel and their love for all that is free and open. This education is concerned with developing an intercultural approach in all school settings: relationships between individuals, the view taken of human knowledge in its totality and in the various academic disciplines, and everyone's integration and rights.

An indispensable condition for co-operation is openness to plurality and differences. Experience shows that the Catholic religion knows how to encounter, respect and esteem different cultures. The love for all men and women is necessarily also a love for their culture. Catholic schools are, by their very vocation, intercultural.

62. Catholic schools' educational programme foresees an harmonious meeting and merging of study and life. This allows students to enjoy a quality formative experience, enriched by intellectual research in the various branches of knowledge and, at the same time, a source of wisdom due to its context: life nourished by the Gospel. In this way, one

avoids the risk of an education that fails, in the first place, to foster the individual's whole formation. In fact, "school is one of the educational environments in which we develop through learning how to live, how to become grown-up, mature men and women who can travel, who can follow the road of life … It helps you not only by developing your intelligence, but also by an integral formation of all the aspects of your personality."[59]

63. The educational programme's principal areas of attention are the following:

The criterion of Catholic identity. The goal of Catholic schools, in all their forms, is to live in fidelity to their educational mission, which has Christ as its foundation. "The fact that in their own individual ways all members of the school community share this Christian vision, makes the school 'Catholic'; principles of the Gospel in this manner become the educational norms since the school then has them as its internal motivation and final goal."[60] This explicit identity gives meaning to the school's other responsibilities.

Building up a common vision. Education can help identify within itself whatever is essential and universal, uniting individuals in their differences. The role of education today is precisely to promote dialogue, enabling communication between different people, helping them to "translate" their different ways of thinking and feeling. This is not just a matter of carrying forward dialogue as a process or method. It is a question, rather, of helping people to revisit their own cultures, with the cultures of others as their starting-point: in other words, helping people to reflect on themselves within a perspective of "openness to humanity".

Reasoned openness to globalization. An educating community like the school should not form people to be parochial. Instead, it should offer students the knowledge necessary to understand man's current condition, as citizen of the whole planet, a condition characterized by numerous relationships of interdependency.

One seeks to *form strong personal identities*, which are not in opposition to each other. In fact, an awareness of one's own tradition and culture is the starting-point from which one can dialogue and recognize the equal dignity of the other person.

Self-awareness is developed by habitually rethinking one's own experiences; reflecting on one's own behaviour; and becoming more self-aware, including by means of cognitive strategies and formation away from self-centredness.

The values of other cultures and religions must be respected and understood. Schools must become places of pluralism, where one learns to dialogue about the *meanings* that people of different religions attribute to their respective signs. This allows one to share universal values, such as solidarity, tolerance and freedom.

One educates to sharing and responsibility. Schools must not be a hiatus in life, purely artificial places dedicated solely to developing the cognitive dimension. While respecting the students' individual timeframes for reaching maturity as well as their personal freedom, schools must assume responsibility for helping the students to understand life's social and cultural situations. Schools must also encourage the students to take on responsibility for improving these situations. Moreover, given schools' attention to the whole person and to all human experience, they do not limit their responsibilities to the merely didactic. Schools also care for many other aspects of the students' lives, in informal ways (parties, fun moments, etc.), formal ways (presentations from informed guest speakers, discussion times, etc.) and religious experiences (times for liturgy and spirituality, etc.).[61]

The Curriculum as the Expression of the School's Identity

64. The curriculum is how the school community makes explicit its goals and objectives, the content of its teaching and the means for communicating it effectively. In the

curriculum, the school's cultural and pedagogical identity are made manifest. Developing the curriculum is one of the school's most demanding tasks, because here one makes explicit what are the school's reference values, subject priorities and practical choices.

65. For a Catholic school, examining its curriculum leads to strengthening what is specific to its nature. It means strengthening the particular way it serves individuals, using the tools offered by culture. Thus, the school's programmes can be effectively harmonized with the school's original mission. One cannot be content merely with an up-to-date didactic offering that simply responds to the demands deriving from the ever-changing economic situation. Catholic schools think out their curricula to place centre-stage both individuals and their search for meaning. This is the reference value, in view of which the various academic disciplines are important resources and take on greater value to the extent that they are tools for educating. From this perspective, what is taught is not neutral, and neither is the way of teaching it.

66. It has been said that we live in a knowledge-based society. However, Catholic schools are encouraged to promote a wisdom-based society, to go beyond knowledge and educate people to think, evaluating facts in the light of values. They educate people to take on responsibility and duties, and exercise active citizenship. Among matters taught specifically in Catholic schools, pride of place must be given to the knowledge of different cultures, with attention given to helping the students encounter and compare the various cultures' many different viewpoints. The curriculum must help the students reflect on the great problems of our time, including those where one sees more clearly the difficult situation of a large part of humanity's living conditions. These would include the unequal distribution of resources, poverty, injustice and human rights denied. "Poverty" implies a careful consideration of the phenomenon of globalization, and suggests a broad and

developed vision of poverty, in all its various forms and causes.[62]

67. A good curriculum can merge theoretical lessons with presentations from informed speakers, where life-experiences are presented in light of faith's view of the world. A good curriculum can also contain practical experiences for sharing and assuming responsibilities.

The two poles are directed towards each other: lessons are informed by hearing about the life-experiences; knowledge becomes experience; and experience acquires the force of a cultural offering, of proclamation.

In teaching the various academic disciplines, teachers share and promote a methodological viewpoint in which the various branches of knowledge are dynamically correlated, in a wisdom perspective. The epistemological framework of every branch of knowledge has its own identity, both in content and methodology. However, this framework does not relate merely to "internal" questions, touching upon the correct realization of each discipline. Each discipline is not an island inhabited by a form of knowledge that is distinct and ring-fenced; rather, it is in a dynamic relationship with all other forms of knowledge, each of which expresses something about the human person and touches upon some truth.

68. Schools are challenged by the multicultural make-up of their classes. They must be able to rethink what is taught; the learning methods; their own internal organization, roles and relationships with families; and the social and cultural context where they are to be found. A curriculum that is open to the intercultural perspective presents the students with a study of civilizations that were previously unknown to them, or were remote from them, but which now are brought to their attention, as well as being brought much "closer" thanks to globalization and modern means of communication, crossing barriers of space and ideological defences. Teaching that aims to help students understand the reality in which they live cannot ignore the aspect of

encounter. On the contrary, teaching has the duty to favour dialogue, as well as cultural and spiritual exchanges.
69. On the didactic level, schools must present their own intercultural concerns while remembering the two levels of learning: the cognitive and the relational-affective. On the cognitive level, schools develop the contents of the curriculum: areas of knowledge to be taught and skills to be promoted. On the relational-affective level, schools develop attitudes and ways of talking about others, teaching the students to respect diversity and take different viewpoints into account, cultivating empathy and collaboration.

Teaching the Catholic Religion

70. In today's context, human societies seek to give themselves broader, trans-national structures, moving towards a system of global *governance*. Moreover, the immense *symbolic patrimonies* that different peoples have built, defended and handed down for centuries, through their specific cultural and religious traditions, seem to be ignored in their true humanizing capacity; instead, they become reasons for separation, in mutual diffidence. Therefore, the biggest challenge in intercultural education lies ever more in the dialogue between one's own identity and other visions of life.
71. Today's cultural shift shows clear signs of oscillation between dialogue and conflict. Especially when faced with this crisis of direction, then, the contribution of Christians is seen to be indispensable. Therefore, it is fundamental that the Catholic religion, for its part, be an inspiring sign of dialogue. In fact, it can be stated absolutely that the Christian message has never been so universal and fundamental as today.
72. Therefore, religion passes on the witness and message of integral humanism. This humanism, enriched by religion's identity, appreciates religion's great traditions such as: faith; respect for human life from conception until its natural end; and respect for the family, for community, for education and for work. These are opportunities and tools

not of closure but of openness and dialogue with everyone and everything, leading to what is good and true. Dialogue remains the only possible solution, even when faced with the denial of religious sentiment, with atheism and agnosticism.

73. From this perspective, teaching the Catholic religion in schools takes on a meaningful role.[63] Primarily, it is a question of the right to education, based on an anthropological understanding of men and women that is open to the transcendent. Together with moral formation, it also helps to develop personal and social responsibility, as well as the other civic virtues, for the common good of society. The Second Vatican Council recalls that "parents, moreover, have the right to determine, in accordance with their own religious beliefs, the kind of religious education that their children are to receive ... The rights of parents are violated, if their children are forced to attend lessons or instructions which are not in agreement with their religious beliefs, or if a single system of education, from which all religious formation is excluded, is imposed upon all."[64] This statement is echoed in the *Universal Declaration of Human Rights*[65] as well as in other declarations and conventions of the international community.[66]

74. Moreover, it must be pointed out that teaching the Catholic religion in schools has its own aims, different from those of catechesis. In fact, while catechesis promotes personal adherence to Christ and maturing of the Christian life, school teaching gives the students knowledge about Christianity's identity and the Christian life. Thus, one aims "'to enlarge the area of our rationality, to reopen it to the larger questions of the truth and the good, to link theology, philosophy and science between them in full respect for the methods proper to them and for their reciprocal autonomy, but also in the awareness of the intrinsic unity that holds them together'. The religious dimension is in fact intrinsic to culture. It contributes to the overall formation of the person and makes it possible to transform knowledge into

wisdom of life." Therefore, with the teaching of the Catholic religion, "school and society are enriched with true laboratories of culture and humanity in which, by deciphering the significant contribution of Christianity, the person is equipped to discover goodness and to grow in responsibility, to seek comparisons and to refine his or her critical sense, to draw from the gifts of the past to understand the present better and to be able to plan wisely for the future."[67] Finally, it counts that the teaching of religion is a field of study in schools. This gives it *status*, placing it alongside the other disciplines in the school's curriculum, in a necessary interdisciplinary dialogue and not as a mere appendix.

75. Consequently, the twin aims of broadening what reason engages and supporting interdisciplinary and intercultural dialogue can be effectively promoted by a confessional teaching of religion. In fact, "if religious education is limited to a presentation of the different religions, in a comparative and 'neutral' way, it creates confusion or generates religious relativism or indifferentism."[68]

The Formation of Teachers and Administrators

76. The formation of teachers and administrators is of crucial importance. In most countries, the state provides the initial formation of school personnel. Good though this may be, it cannot be considered sufficient. In fact, Catholic schools bring something extra, particular to them, that must always be recognized and developed. Therefore, while the obligatory formation needs to consider those disciplinary and professional matters typical of teaching and administrating, it must also consider the cultural and pedagogical fundamentals that make up Catholic schools' identity.

77. The time spent in formation must be used for reinforcing the idea of Catholic schools as being communities of fraternal relationships and places of research, dedicated to deepening and communicating truth in the various scholarly disciplines. Those who have leadership positions are duty-bound to guarantee that all personnel receive adequate preparation to serve effectively. Moreover, they must

serve in coherence with the faith they profess, and be able to interpret society's demands in the actual situation of its current configuration.[69] This also favours the school's collaboration with parents in education,[70] respecting their responsibility as first and natural educators.[71]

78. Formation that is particularly dedicated to promoting sensitivity, awareness and competence in the intercultural field can be advanced by paying attention to the following three essential markers:

a) *integration*: this has to do with the school's ability to be adequately prepared for receiving students of different cultural backgrounds, responding to their needs regarding scholastic achievement and personal enhancement;

b) *interaction*: this has to do with knowing how to facilitate good relationships among peers and among adults. There is an awareness that simply being in the same physical environment is not enough. Encouragement must be given to curiosity about other people, openness and friendship, both in class and in places and times outside the school. Thus, situations of distancing between people, discrimination and conflict can be avoided and repaired.

c) *recognizing the other person*: one must avoid falling into the trap of imposing one's own views on the other person, asserting one's own lifestyle and one's own way of thinking without taking into account the other person's culture and particular emotional situation.

79. One must pursue the task of promoting unity, on the cultural level, among the various branches of knowledge. This means overcoming compartmentalization and abstraction, searching instead for meaning in its broader sense. It is no less important, indeed it is essential, for the educational community to task itself with overcoming compartmentalization in relationships—of interpersonal, communitarian and collective natures. Where there is no awareness of unity—in the richness of diversity, of both the individual and society—there can be no development of knowledge that is

wholly "human", and not merely functional—knowledge that both preserves tradition and is open to innovation.

80. Catholic schools develop, in a manner wholly particular to them, the basic hypothesis that formation covers the whole arc of professional experience and is not limited to the period of initial formation or formation in the early years. Catholic schools require people not only to know how to teach or direct an organization; they also require them, using the skills of their profession, to know how to bear authentic witness to the school's values, as well as to their own continuing efforts to live out ever more deeply, in thought and deed, the ideals that are stated publicly in words.

Hence, it is important that schools know how to be communities of formation and of study, where relationships among individuals colour relationships among academic disciplines. Knowledge is enhanced from within by this reclaimed unity, in the light of the Gospel and Christian doctrine, and so can make its own essential contribution to the integral growth of both individuals and the evermore heralded global society.

Being Teachers, Being Administrators

81. Formation is always guided by how one defines the professions involved in education. Therefore, one must answer the questions: what does it mean to be a teacher; what does it mean to be an administrator in a Catholic school? What are the areas of expertise that must characterize these professions?

82. Teachers today are members of a professional community. They contribute to writing the curriculum; and they have responsibility for relationships with various other subjects, especially the students' families. A good school is where the teachers, as a group, know how to become something more than a mere recognized *corps*, in which the members are bound together by ties of mere bureaucracy. Instead, they should be a community, living out professional and personal relationships not just on a superficial

level, but on a much deeper level, bound together by a shared concern for education.

83. Good teachers know that their responsibilities do not end outside the classroom or school. They know that their responsibilities are also connected with their local area, and are demonstrated by their understanding for today's social problems. Professional preparation and technical competence are necessary prerequisites for teaching, but they are not enough. An expression of education lies in helping young people to understand their own time and plan their lives around a credible premise. Multiculturalism and pluralism are characteristic traits of our times; thus, teachers must be able to provide their students with the cultural tools necessary for giving direction to their lives. Moreover, teachers must allow their students, in the routine of the classroom, to experience real listening, respect, dialogue and the value of diversity.

84. Being ever more multicultural, schools are tasked with helping people with different experiences to relate to each other. Schools must also act as mediators between such people. People's different experiences need to be acknowledged and recognized. Teachers and school administrators require new professional skills, aimed at reconciling differences, allowing them to dialogue with each other. Teachers and school administrators need to offer shared perspectives, while respecting the individual nature of different people's development and world visions.

85. For those who occupy positions of leadership, there can be a strong temptation to consider the school like a company or business. However, schools that aim to be educating communities need those who govern them to be able to invoke the school's reference values; they must then direct all the school's professional and human resources in this direction. School leaders are more than just managers of an organization. They are true educational leaders when they are the first to take on this responsibility, which is also an ecclesial and pastoral mission rooted in a relationship

with the Church's pastors. School leaders have the particular duty of providing what support is necessary for spreading the culture of dialogue, encounter and mutual recognition between different cultures. Both inside and outside the school, they promote all possible forms of collaboration that help to realize intercultural harmony.

86. So that schools can develop as professional communities, it is necessary that their members learn to reflect and seek together. Schools are communities of shared practices, of communality of ideas and research.

Moreover, the union of the educating community is fostered by strong ties with the Christian community. In fact, Catholic schools are ecclesial subjects. "This ecclesial dimension is not a mere adjunct, but is a proper and specific attribute, a distinctive characteristic which penetrates and informs every moment of its educational activity, a fundamental part of its very identity and the focus of its mission."[72] Therefore, "the whole Christian community, and particularly the diocesan Ordinary, bear the responsibility 'of arranging everything so that all the faithful have a Catholic education' (c. 794 §2 CIC) and, more precisely, of having 'schools which offer an education imbued with a Christian spirit' (c. 802 CIC; cf. c. 635 CCEO)."[73] The ecclesial nature of Catholic schools, which is inscribed in the very heart of their identity as schools, is the reason for "the institutional link they keep with the Church hierarchy, which guarantees that the instruction and education be grounded in the principles of the Catholic faith and imparted by teachers of right doctrine and probity of life (cf. c. 803 CIC; cc. 632 e 639 CCEO)."[74]

CONCLUSION

The tradition of Catholic schools is familiar with the intercultural aspect. Today, however, faced with the challenges both of globalization and of cultural and religious pluralism, it is essential to develop a greater awareness of its meaning. In this way, Catholic schools will communicate better—in their presence, witness and teaching—their own particular way of being, being *Catholic*. They are schools that are open to the universality of knowledge and, at the same time, have their own specific nature, which comes from their being rooted in their believing in Christ the Teacher and their belonging to the Church.

Catholic schools avoid both fundamentalism and ideas of relativism where everything is the same. Instead, they are encouraged to progress in harmony with the identity they have received from their Gospel inspiration. They are also invited to follow the pathways that lead to encountering others. They educate themselves, and they educate to dialogue, which consists in speaking with everyone and relating to everyone with respect, esteem and listening in sincerity. They should express themselves with authenticity, without obfuscating or watering down their own vision so as to acquire greater consensus. They should bear witness by means of their own presence, as well as by the coherence between what they say and what they do.

To all educators we want to address the encouraging and guiding words of Pope Francis: "Do not be disheartened in the face of the difficulties that the educational challenge presents! Educating is not a profession but an attitude, a way of being; in order to educate it is necessary to step out of ourselves and be among young people, to accompany them in the stages of their growth and to set ourselves beside them. Give them hope and optimism for their journey in the world. Teach them to see the beauty and goodness of creation and of man who always retains the Creator's hallmark. But above all with your life be witnesses of what you communicate. Educators … pass on knowledge and values with their words; but their words will have an incisive effect on children and young people if they are accompanied by their witness, their consistent way of life. Without consistency it is impossible to educate! You are all educators, there are no delegates in this field. Thus collaboration in a spirit of unity and community among the various educators is essential and must be fostered and encouraged. School can and must be a catalyst, it must be a place of encounter and convergence of the entire educating community, with the sole objective of training and helping to develop mature people who are simple, competent and honest, who know how to love with fidelity, who can live life as a response to God's call, and their future profession as a service to society."[75]

The Holy Father Pope Francis has given his approval for the publication of this document.
Rome, 28 October 2013, 48th anniversary of the promulgation of the Second Vatican Council's Declaration *Gravissimum Educationis*.

Zenon Cardinal Grocholewski, *Prefect*
Archbishop Angelo Vincenzo Zani, *Secretary*

Notes

1 Cf. UNESCO, *Convention on the Protection and Promotion of the Diversity of Cultural Expressions,* Paris (20 October 2005), art. 4.

2 Cf. Congregation for Catholic Education, *The Catholic School on the Threshold of the Third Millennium* (28 December 1997), n. 3.

3 John XXIII, Encyclical Letter *Pacem in Terris* (11 April 1963), n. 9.

4 Pontifical Council for Interreligious Dialogue; Congregation for the Evangelization of Peoples, Instruction *Dialogue and Proclamation: Reflection and Orientations on Interreligious Dialogue and the Proclamation of the Gospel of Jesus Christ* (19 May 1991), n. 45.

5 John Paul II, *Speech to the Italian Church* (Palermo, 23 November 1995), n. 4.

6 Second Vatican Council, *Declaration on the Relations of the Church to Non-Christian Religions* Nostra Aetate (28 October 1965), n. 1.

7 Cf. Pontifical Council for Culture; Pontifical Council for Interreligious Dialogue, *Jesus Christ the Bearer of the Water of Life: A Christian Reflection on the "New Age"* (Vatican City 2003).

8 Cf. Benedict XVI, Encyclical Letter *Caritas in Veritate* (29 January 2009), nn. 55-56.

9 *Ibid.*, n. 56.

10 *Ibid.*

11 John Paul II, *Speech to the Plenary Session of the Pontifical Council for Culture* (18 January 1983), n. 7.

12 Benedict XVI, *Speech to Religious Leaders in the Notre Dame Centre of Jerusalem* (11 May 2009).

13 Cf. Congregation for the Doctrine of the Faith, *Declaration* Dominus Iesus *on the Unicity and Salvific Universality of Jesus Christ and the Church* (6 August 2000), n. 7. The International Theological Commission underlined how interreligious dialogue is "connatural to the Christian vocation. It is inscribed in the dynamism of the living tradition of the mystery of salvation, whose universal sacrament is the Church" (*Christianity and the World Religions*, 30 September 1997, n. 114). As an expression of this tradition, interreligious dialogue is not an individual or private initiative, because "it is not Christians who are sent, but the Church; it is not their ideas that they present but Christ's; it will not be their rhetoric that will touch hearts but the Spirit, the Paraclete. To be faithful to the 'sense of the Church', the interreligious dialogue begs for the humility of Christ and the transparency of the Holy Spirit" (*Idem*, n. 116).

14 Benedict XVI, *Speech to Religious Leaders in the Notre Dame Centre of Jerusalem*.

15 Cf. Second Vatican Council, *Decree on Ecumenism* Unitatis Redintegratio (24 November 1964), n. 4.

16 Benedict XVI, *Speech to the Diplomatic Corps Accredited to the Holy See* (7 January 2008).

17 Congregation for the Doctrine of the Faith, *Declaration* Dominus Iesus *on the Unicity and Salvific Universality of Jesus Christ and the Church*, n. 15.

18 Benedict XVI, *Speech to Representatives of Other Religions* (Washington DC, 17 April 2008).

19 Congregation for Catholic Education, *The Catholic School* (19 March 1977), n. 33.

20 John Paul II, *Apostolic Exhortation* Ecclesia in Africa (14 September 1995), n. 102.

21 Pope Francis, *Speech to the Students of the Jesuit Schools of Italy and Albania* (7 June 2013).

22 John Paul II, *Dialogue Between Cultures for a Civilization of Love and Peace*, Message for the World Day of Peace (2001), n. 20.

23 John Paul II, *Dialogue Between Cultures for a Civilization of Love and Peace*, n. 20.

24 Pontifical Council for Interreligious Dialogue; Congregation for the Evangelization of Peoples, Instruction *Dialogue and Proclamation: Reflection and Orientations on Interreligious Dialogue and the Proclamation of the Gospel of Jesus Christ*, n. 46.

25 Pope Francis, *Speech to Students and Teachers of the Seibu Gakuen Bunry Junior High School of Saitama, Tokyo* (21 August 2013).

26 Cf. Council of Europe, *White Paper on Intercultural Dialogue "Living Together as Equals in Dignity"*, Strasburg (May 2008), p. 5: "the intercultural approach offers a forward-looking model for managing cultural diversity. It proposes a conception based on individual human dignity (embracing our common humanity and common destiny)."

27 Benedict XVI. Encyclical Letter *Caritas in Veritate*, n. 26.

28 *Ibid*.

29 *Ibid*.

30 Second Vatican Council, Pastoral Constitution on the Church in the Modern World *Gaudium et Spes* (7 December 1965) n. 53.

31 John Paul II, *Speech to UNESCO*, Paris (2 June 1980), n. 6.

32 Second Vatican Council, Pastoral Constitution on the Church in the Modern World *Gaudium et Spes*, n. 53.

33 *Ibid*.

34 John Paul II, *Dialogue Between Cultures for a Civilization of Love And Peace*, nn. 7 and 9.

35 Cf. International Theological Commission, *Faith and Inculturation* (8 October 1988), Chap. I—Nature, Culture and Grace, n. 7.

36 John Paul II, *Dialogue Between Cultures for a Civilization of Love And Peace*, nn. 10 and 16.

37 Congregation for Catholic Education, *Educating Together in Catholic Schools: A Shared Mission Between Consecrated Persons and the Lay Faithful* (8 September 2007), n. 8.

38 Second Vatican Council, Dogmatic Constitution *Lumen Gentium* (21 November 1964), n. 1.

39 Second Vatican Council, Pastoral Constitution *Gaudium et Spes*, n. 22.

40 John Paul II, Encyclical Letter *Fides et Ratio* (14 September 1998), n. 70.

41 Cf. Benedict XVI, *Speech to the General Assembly of the Italian Bishops' Conference* (27 May 2010): "the essential fact is that the human person becomes himself only with the other. The 'I' becomes itself only from the 'thou' and from the 'you'. It is created for dialogue, for synchronic and diachronic communion. It is only the encounter with the 'you' and with the 'we' that the 'I' opens to itself."

42 Benedict XVI, Encyclical Letter *Caritas in Veritate*, n. 53.

43 *Ibid*., n. 54.

44 Cf. *Ibid*., n. 55.

45 Second Vatican Council, Pastoral Constitution *Gaudium et Spes*, n. 12.

46 Benedict XVI, Encyclical Letter *Caritas in Veritate*, n. 53.

47 John Paul II, Encyclical Letter *Redemptor Hominis* (4 March 1979), n. 10.

48 Benedict XVI, Encyclical Letter *Deus Caritas Est* (25 December 2005), n. 6.

49 Benedict XVI, Encyclical Letter *Caritas in Veritate,* n. 53.

50 Cf. John Paul II, Apostolic Letter *Novo Millennio Ineunte* (6 January 2001), n. 43.

51 Cf. International Theological Commission, *In Search of a Universal Ethic: A New Look at the Natural Law* (2009), n. 51: " 'Do not do to another that which you would not want done to you'. Here we encounter the golden rule, which today is posited as the very principle of a morality of reciprocity."

52 Congregation for the Doctrine of the Faith, *Doctrinal Note on Some Aspects of Evangelization* (3 December 2007), n. 7.

53 Cf. Congregation for Catholic Education, *The Catholic School on the Threshold of the Third Millennium,* n. 3.

54 Benedict XVI, *Blessed are the Peacemakers,* Message for the World Day of Peace (2013), n. 4.

55 Cf. Congregation for Catholic Education, *Educating Together in Catholic Schools: A Shared Mission Between Consecrated Persons and the Lay Faithful,* n. 38.

56 Cf. Congregation for Catholic Education, *The Catholic School,* nn. 33-37.

57 Cf. Congregation for Catholic Education, *Lay Catholics in Schools: Witnesses to Faith* (15 October 1982), n. 22; Id., *Educating Together in Catholic Schools: A Shared Mission Between Consecrated Persons and the Lay Faithful,* n. 13.

58 Congregation for Catholic Education, *The Religious Dimension of Education in a Catholic School* (7 April 1988), n. 42.

59 Pope Francis, *Speech to the Students of the Jesuit Schools of Italy and Albania.*

60 Congregation for Catholic Education, *The Catholic School,* n. 34; cf. Code of Canon Law, can. 803 § 2.

61 Pope Francis, addressing the Jesuits that run schools, encouraged them "to seek new forms of non-conventional education in accordance with 'the needs of the times and of people'" (7 June 2013).

62 Cf. Benedict XVI, *Fighting Poverty to Build Peace,* Message for the World Day of Peace (2009), n. 2.

63 Cf. Congregation for Catholic Education, *Circular Letter to the Presidents of Bishops' Conferences on Religious Education in Schools* (5 May 2009).

64 Second Vatican Council, Declaration *Dignitatis Humanae* (7 December 1965), n. 5; cf. Code of Canon Law, can. 799; cf. also Holy See, *Charter of the Rights of the Family* (22 October 1983), art. 5, c-d.

65 Cf. United Nations, *Universal Declaration of Human Rights* (1948), art. 26.

66 Cf., e.g., *Additional Protocol n. 1 to the European Convention for the Protection of Human Rights and Fundamental Freedoms* (1952), art. 2; United Nations, *Declaration of the Rights of the Child* (1959), principle 7, 2; UNESCO, *Convention Against Discrimination in Education* (1960), art. 5, b; United Nations, *Convention on the Rights of the Child* (1989), art. 18, 1.

67 Benedict XVI, *Speech to Catholic Religion Teachers* (25 April 2009).

68 Congregation for Catholic Education, *Circular Letter to the Presidents of Bishops' Conferences on Religious Education in Schools*, n. 12.

69 Cf. Congregation for Catholic Education, *Educating Together in Catholic Schools: A Shared Mission Between Consecrated Persons and the Lay Faithful* (8 September 2007), nn. 34-37.

70 Cf. Code of Canon Law, can. 796 § 1.

71 Cf. Congregation for Catholic Education, *The Religious Dimension of Education in a Catholic School*, n. 32; cf. also Code of Canon Law, can. 799.

72 Congregation for Catholic Education, *The Catholic School on the Threshold of the Third Millennium*, n. 11.

73 Congregation for Catholic Education, *Circular Letter to the Presidents of Bishops' Conferences on Religious Education in Schools*, n. 5.

74 *Ibid.*, n. 6.

75 Pope Francis, Speech to the Students of the Jesuit Schools of Italy and Albania.

Appendix 2

Pope Francis

Address to Participants in the Plenary Session of the Congregation for Catholic Education (For Educational Institutions)

13 February 2014

Dear Cardinals, Venerable Brothers in the Episcopate and in the Priesthood, Dear Brothers and Sisters,

I extend a special welcome to the Cardinals and Bishops who were recently appointed members of this Congregation, and I thank the Cardinal Prefect for the words with which he introduced this meeting.

The topics on your agenda are challenging, indeed, such as updating the Apostolic Constitution *Sapientia Christiana*, strengthening the identity of Catholic universities and preparing for anniversaries that are coming in 2015, such as the 50th anniversary of the Conciliar Declaration *Gravissimum Educationis* and the 25th anniversary of the Apostolic Constitution *Ex Corde Ecclesiae*. Catholic education is one of the most important challenges for the Church, engaged as she is today in implementing the new evangelization in a historical and cultural context which is in constant flux. In this perspective, I would like to draw your attention to three aspects.

The first aspect concerns the *importance of dialogue in education*. Of late, you have developed the theme of an education for intercultural dialogue in Catholic schools with the publication of a specific document. In fact, Catholic schools and universities are attended by many non-Christian students as well as non-believers. Catholic educational institutions offer everyone an education aimed at the integral development of the person that responds to right of all people to have access to knowledge and understanding. But they are equally called to offer to all the Christian message—respecting fully the freedom of all and the proper methods of each specific scholastic environment—namely that Jesus Christ is the meaning of life, of the cosmos and of history.

Jesus began to preach the Good News in the "Galilee of the Gentiles", a crossroads for people of different races, cultures and religions. In some ways this context is similar to today's world. The profound changes that have led to the ever spreading multicultural societies requires those who work in schools and universities to become involved in the educational programmes of exchange and dialogue, with a bold and innovative fidelity able to bring together the Catholic identity to meet the different "souls" existing in a multicultural society. I think with appreciation of the contribution which religious institutions and other ecclesial institutes offer through the foundation and management of Catholic schools in contexts strongly marked by cultural and religious pluralism.

The second aspect is the *quality preparation of formators*. We cannot improvise. We must take this seriously. In the meeting I had with the Superiors General, I underlined that today education is directed at a *changing* generation and, therefore, every educator—and the entire Church who is the mother educator—is called "*to change*", or know how to communicate with the young people before them.

I would like to limit myself to recalling the features of an educator and his or her specific duty. To educate is an act of love, it is to give life. And love is demanding, it calls for the best resources, for a reawakening of the passion to begin this path patiently with young people. The educator in Catholic schools must be, first and foremost, competent and qualified but, at the same time, someone who is rich in humanity and capable of being with young people in a style of pedagogy that helps promote their human and spiritual growth. Youth are in need of quality teaching along with values that are not only articulated but witnessed to. Consistency is an indispensable factor in the education of young people! Consistency! We cannot grow and we cannot educate without consistency: consistency and witness!

For this, an educator is himself in need of permanent formation. It is necessary to invest so that teachers and supervisors may maintain a high level of professionalism and also maintain their faith and the strength of their spiritual impetus. And in this permanent formation too I would suggest a need for retreats and spiritual exercises for educators. It is a beautiful thing to offer courses on the subject, but it is also necessary to offer spiritual exercises and retreats focused on prayer! For consistency requires effort but most of all it is a gift and a grace. We must ask for it!

The last aspect concerns *educational institutions*, that is, schools and Catholic and ecclesial universities. The 50th anniversary of the Conciliar Declaration, the 25th anniversary of *Ex Corde Ecclesiae* and the updating of *Sapientia Christiana* lead us to reflect seriously on the many formational institutions around the world and on their duty to be an expression of a living presence of the Gospel in the field of education, of science and of culture. Catholic academic institutions cannot isolate themselves from the world, they must know how to enter bravely into the areopagus of current culture and open dialogue, conscious of the gift that they can offer to everyone.

Dear ones, education is a great open building site in which the Church has always been present through her institutions and projects. Today we must encourage this commitment on all levels and renew the commitment of all engaged in the new evangelization. On this horizon, I thank you all for your work and I invoke through the intercession of the Virgin Mary the perpetual help of the Holy Spirit for you and your work. I ask you to please pray for me and for my ministry. And from my heart, I bless you. Thank you!

CONTRIBUTORS

Ronnie Convery is a journalist and broadcaster. He has written for newspapers and journals in the UK and Italy and has spoken at international conferences on themes relating to religion and communication. After studies at the Universities of Glasgow MA (Hons) and *La Sapienza* (Rome), he embarked on a career in newspaper and TV journalism before being appointed Director of Communications of the Archdiocese of Glasgow. Ronnie is the founder and editor of the on-line journal *Italian Scotland* and author of *The Cardinal*—the official tribute to Cardinal Thomas Winning of the Archdiocese of Glasgow. In 2008 Ronnie was named a Cavaliere of the Italian Republic by President Giorgio Napolitano in recognition of his many years of services to the Italian community abroad.

Leonardo Franchi is a lecturer in religious education at the University of Glasgow where he is currently Head of the St. Andrew's Foundation and Director of Catholic Teacher Education. He is involved in teaching aspects of religious education at both undergraduate and masters level. Leonardo has degrees from the University of Glasgow (MA (Hons) and PhD) and the Maryvale Institute (MEd). He is the editor of *An Anthology of Catholic Teaching on Education* (Scepter UK) and, with Stephen McKinney, *A Companion to Catholic Education* (Gracewing).

Raymond McCluskey studied at Glasgow (MA) and Oxford (DPhil) Universities. After temporary lectureships in History at the Universities of St Andrews and Edinburgh, he completed a PGCE and taught in secondary education for over a decade at the Jesuit school in Glasgow. In 2004, he joined the Faculty (now School) of Education in the University of Glasgow where he is currently a University

Teacher. Raymond has previously edited *The See of Ninian* (Ayr, 1997), *The Scots College, Rome* (Edinburgh, 2000) and (with Stephen McKinney) *How "The Teacher" is presented in Literature, History, Religion, and the Arts* (Lewiston NY, 2013).

Robert Davis is Professor of Religious and Cultural Education at the University of Glasgow and was Head of the School of Education from 2010-2014. Robert has degrees from Strathclyde (BA) and Stirling universities (MLitt, PhD). He continues to teach across a range of undergraduate and post-graduate programmes in Initial Teacher Education. Robert has published widely in many fields, including childhood studies, Robert Owen studies and Catholic education. He was a joint author of *Does Religious Education Work? A Multi-Dimensional Education,* published by Bloomsbury in 2013, and a volume (with Dr Francis O'Hagan) on Robert Owen, published in 2010 as part of the Continuum Library of Educational Thought.

Lightning Source UK Ltd.
Milton Keynes UK
UKOW03f0601220814

237337UK00001B/9/P